Marcel Lucont des̶ raconteur and bon v̶ a cult following on the in̶ scene with his trademark sardonic mus̶... sharp wit and his louche poetry. Winner of the Buxton Fringe Award 2009 for Best Comedy Individual and the Three Weeks Editors' Choice Award at Edinburgh 2008, he considers himself the best French comedian on the UK circuit today.

www.marcellucont.com

First published in 2011 by New Holland Publishers (UK) Ltd
London • Cape Town • Sydney • Auckland
www.newhollandpublishers.com

Garfield House, 86–88 Edgware Road, London W2 2EA, United Kingdom
80 McKenzie Street, Cape Town 8001, South Africa
Unit 1, 66 Gibbes Street, Chatswood, NSW 2067, Australia
218 Lake Road, Northcote, Auckland, New Zealand

2 4 6 8 10 9 7 5 3 1

Publisher: Aruna Vasudevan
Senior Editor: Charlotte Macey
Senior Production Controller: Melanie Dowland
Design and illustration: Colin Hall – www.typefunction.co.uk

Reproduction by PDQ Digital Media Solutions Ltd, United Kingdom
Printed and bound in India by Replika Press

what we French think of you British

think of you

British

...And Where You Are Going Wrong

Marcel Lucont

NEW
HOLLAND

CONTENTS

CULTURE AND CUISINE

THE ENGLISH LANGUAGE

Introduction

I can only imagine how excited you must be to hold this book in your hand. This, my first book in the English language. A book, appropriately, about Britain, and its myriad wrongs. If you, reader, are British, expect to face some home truths. They may be ugly, but trust me, I am holding up this verbal mirror to your ruddied faces only to help you to better yourselves.

You are welcome.

It contains observations, suggestions, poetry and pictorials. There may also be, in the spirit of Proust, lengthy sentences which, just as you think they are about to end, continue, ever-evolving, as a Frenchman's stream of thought has a tendency to do, flowing calmly and intellectually through an undulating sea of existential postulation, moral dichotomy and social examination, perhaps to some logical conclusion, perhaps (as is more often the case), to a wider ocean of possibility, upon which a new horizon rests, stretching sublimely to infinity.

Do not fear these sentences. If you have read this far, already you have a greater span of concentration than most Britons, and are worthy of this book. Well done.

When you have finished the book, wrap it in fabric, place it in a brass tin and store it as far underground as you can dig before it inevitably begins to rain. It is a limited edition. Everything is. Including you.

Yes, apologies for this 'spoiler', but eventually every one of us will die. Therefore, you may as well spend your time engaged in wholesome pursuits, such as reading this book in its entirety.

And why am I passing this valuable information on to you, perhaps you ask?

For the money and adoration, mainly, but also to help curb the troubling advance of American culture on your isle. Yes, in the American style they have removed their Bush, but at this stage it is like keeping a dog inside only after it has defecated on every neighbour's lawn, mauled several children and fucked everybody's leg. And invaded Iraq. 'Ah, but now we have Mr Obama,' they say. 'America is "cool" again.' I say, it depends how one defines 'cool.' I say, whose president is fucking a supermodel?

Anyway, I will now wind down this introduction to allow you to enjoy the main thrust of the book. This is your book – enjoy it, obey it, tell others about it. If you are living in Britain, it is the least you deserve.

This is my first full book in this language, so the English may not be entirely perfect, but neither are you.

A large amount of this book was written in the nude.

M Lucont

A Brief History of Marcel

Plus ça change ...

Born: *Roubaix, France, 1979*

Occupation: *flâneur, raconteur, bon viveur*

Marital status: *adulterer*

Hair: *dark brown*

Eyes: *dark green*

Appearance: *dark, handsome*

Religious view: *existential nihilism*

Favourite type of woman: *twins*

Marcel Lucont is easily the finest French raconteur and entertainer working in England today. If you don't believe this, simply ask him yourself. As a self-published, self-award-winning author in his native France, to be published in England is really quite an honour, for you British.

Marcel began life in Roubaix, Northern France, in the traditional way – as a boy. Raised by his father, Gérard, and his various lovers over the years, he never truly knew his mother, who left in Marcel's early years, never to return. Raised at a time when smoking was compulsory in France, Marcel was a natural and by the age of nine could roll a cigarette with one hand while writing poetry with the other.

Despite poor attendance at school and college, Marcel still managed to achieve extraordinarily high grades, due to a combination of reading in his spare time, extra-curricular assistance from some of the younger female members of staff and generally being better than everyone else.

Eventually evicted by his father, due to heated arguments over the theft of cigarettes, alcohol and partners, Marcel moved to Paris to study philosophy at the Sorbonne, where his enormous talents as a performer were also realized.

... plus c'est la même chose

Performances of his now legendary controversial cabaret shows would regularly sell out almost instantly, often featuring biting satire, classic *chansons*, nudity, animals and live fireworks.

Sadly, Marcel's university career was ended prematurely, in 2001, after an incident involving a rogue firework, a cat and a stripper. Unable to persuade the university otherwise, even using philosophy, bribery and seduction, Marcel was forced back to Roubaix, heavily in debt and wanted dead by various animal protection groups and a pimp.

A year later, Marcel's father suffered a fatal heart attack while in bed with his third wife. This came as a shock to the entire town, especially his fourth wife. A speech by Marcel at the funeral involving the phrase '*la petite mort*' did not make the situation any better.

After selling the family apartment, he left his home town and since then the world has been fortunate enough to play host to Marcel Lucont and his wise words of cynicism and honesty in the face of an increasingly stupid and intolerant world.

For the time being, Marcel resides in London. He passes his time talking at various audiences in the theatres, cabaret venues and comedy clubs of the UK and completing his second English-language book, the sex-addiction manual *Thinking Outside The Box*.

He is currently very much at the 'research' stage.

France and England
Setting the Record Straight

Before I begin, it is important to dispel a few myths regarding Anglo–French relations, especially seeing as the majority of English people probably believe the *Entente Cordiale* to be some kind of cocktail.

The French despise the English

A myth – while the English are indeed despised all over the world, the French prefer simply to ignore them. Hatred is a relatively energy-consuming and ultimately worthless emotion and we French have better ways to expend our energy, such as healthy debate, political action, group sex or viniculture. Really, it says something about the big-headed nature of the English that they continually endorse this fabrication.

The French refuse to speak English in France

If this has been your experience in France, you have probably only visited Paris. Perhaps it is your own fault for not expanding your horizons (or learning the language of the country you are in). Even so, it is possible that the French people you encounter are merely holding back their English so as not to embarrass you. They could just as easily speak Italian, Spanish or German to you, just to highlight your inadequacy at learning your one neighbour's language ...

French cleanliness

A bizarre English stereotype of the French is that we are less clean than you. Well, shall we just take back our Yves Saint Laurent, Chanel and Lancôme fragrances that have been keeping English people chic and pleasant to the nasal airways for decades? Often the English will also complain that our toilets are not as well-structured as theirs. Well, personally, I believe one's business in this room should last as short a time as possible. The English, instead, seem to fill theirs with reading material, as though planning an extended stay, hence the importance of throne-like comfort. When it comes to cleanliness, I would argue that the nation choosing to spend more time with their own waste is in fact the more unclean ...

Britannia rules the waves

Well, if one were to visit England and nowhere else, I can see how one would think so, especially during any international football tournament, when the English like to remind everyone what their flag looks like, given *any* opportunity. Thank you for the words *'weekend'* and *'hamburger'*, but I am sure without you we would have found our own names for such things without too much trouble.

The French are a nation of sexual deviants

Well, Monsieur de Sade may perhaps have a little to do with this assumption, although I say it is all relative in a nation where a woman speaking *at all* in a bedroom situation is considered adventurous, and a kiss using the tongue must be known as a 'French kiss'. In France we call it simply 'a kiss'.

France and England   11

'A good society is like good cuisine - it takes just one dick in it to ruin it.'

The British People

It was Sartre, of course, who declared that Hell is other people, a sentiment I completely agree with, having passed the last few months of my life in the city of London, the only place in the world where the phrase 'take care' sounds like a threat. But London, of course, is its own entity – a dirty and increasingly obese child wanting the world to come and play with it but insisting on going to bed at an unreasonably early hour. The rest of Britain contains a plethora of characters, ranging from the stuffy to the opinionated, from the obstinate to the tiresome.

British men

These are curious beings, laughing about things that they have repeated to one another for the fifteenth time, using nicknames that they will often urge you to use too, however well you know them, and ensuring that *everything* in life revolves somehow around alcohol.

The young British male is largely a herd animal, but is also known to roam in packs. An alpha male will make himself known in a variety of ways, which can be seen in towns all over Britain. Alpha male contests include:

- Who can climb the highest public monument.
- Who can sing the loudest into a tiny microphone/traffic cone/vagrant.
- Who can fit the most currency into the hood of their penis.
- Who can punch the most/largest inanimate objects.

Birthdays are seen not as a festival of a young man's achievements thus far in life, but as an opportunity to humiliate him via the means of alcohol, cameras and anything which removes body hair.

There is very little style among British men, who will dress like a teenager for as long as possible, before moving on to nothing but varying shades of brown in later life.

British women

This may sound controversial, but British women could be very attractive. If only they would loosen up, make a little more of an effort in some cases, a lot less in other cases, and stop trying to be British men.

Aspects of femininity in Britain are either eroded or painfully skewed. To borrow an old French observation, 'What do you call a beautiful woman in London? A tourist.'

So many women of Britain are content to look, smell and act plain – a real wasted opportunity on their part. Coco Chanel believed that 'a woman who does not wear perfume has no future.' Mlle Chanel, I believe, was perhaps a little biased in this judgment, but it is still worth noting.

However, Britain also contains plenty of women happy to spread an entire cosmetics range over themselves, with all the subtlety of two circus clowns who have just collided, both carrying buckets of orange paint and glitter.

Loud of mouth

Loud of face

Given the number of fashion magazines consumed by British women, if their newsagents are anything to go by, one would expect a high level of consciousness of fashion and style, but this is not the case. Many of them appear to have chosen clothes at random, including patterns of dizzying complexity. Keep it simple please, ladies. It makes it a lot more difficult for us to undress you mentally when all these lines and shapes are in the way.

The British People

15

Dating in Britain

In France, there is a frisson between the sexes, a kind of aloof dance of desire that is played out daily. In Britain, this dance is more of an awkward waddle. There is a large difference between giving casual looks from afar and doing so to the extent that one appears to be top of a sex offender's register. Dating a British woman is as curious an affair as one would expect, mainly due to a complete disregard for the discussion of politics or philosophy. While often more than happy to reveal a vulgar amount of cleavage, revealing her mind is apparently not the done thing. I have learned via eavesdropping that most date conversations in Britain lean towards the vulgar topics of money, possessions or celebrities, with most couples also having no knowledge of the menu in front of them. Women of Britain are very easy to get into the bedroom, but even I sometimes find the lack of a chase disappointing.

Complimenting a British woman

Be warned that if one chooses to compliment a British woman who has actually made a good job of her appearance and got it just right, she will be surprised – even shocked – that you should choose to do so, especially if no alcohol is involved. It is no wonder that so many turn out to be so unconfident in the bedroom, when they will not even accept compliments in daily life to boost their confidence. And yet, British women are often exceedingly vulgar when talking about sexual matters among themselves, an attribute which, ironically, reduces their sexual attractiveness.

Sex talk

Talking during sex is rare – as is talking after sex. In Britain, intercourse can often feel like a formality, which one must get through with the minimum of vocal input and maximum of alcohol intake. Even among

Britain's atheists, it seems sex is something done with God constantly watching and tutting. It is no wonder so many British women complain of the clumsiness and awkwardness of British men in such situations – they have been given no instructions, and often they are too drunk to remember what they did right or wrong the time before.

Moving in together

When looking for a house to buy, British couples will not only accept a man who will step in, charge extortionate fees and do it for them, but will actively seek out such a man. Property and possessions are so important to the average British couple that they cannot pass an estate agent without cooing at houses they will never be able to afford, and yet they still do business with one of the men who is making them so unaffordable.

They cannot wait to move to their new place, install all the Ikea furniture they can afford with what little money they have remaining and sit down to watch a constant stream of property-based television programmes.

Teenage dating

From what I have seen, the fairground is the Number One place for teenagers to date. There the boy will prove his ineptitude at a range of physical tasks, the girl will feel sick on a ride after too many 'alcopops' and sweets and both will get swindled by gypsies. I will never understand those who defend these people – they call themselves 'travelling folk' and are then angry when people move them on, mainly for ripping off the people of their town.

Raising children

Modern Britain is a terrible place to raise a child. It was suggested in Britain's Victorian era that children should be seen and not heard. Unfortunately, nowadays they are both – to a painful extent. Addicted to television and video games, British children now have the attention spans of wasps, and are just as irritating in public areas.

Chat-up Lines
of the British

Most British men are so inept in the art of procuring women that they fully believe their best option is to consume extraordinary amounts of alcohol, then apply some ill-conceived technique or 'chat-up line' passed on to them by someone equally misguided. British men will say things such as 'Oysters will win a woman every time.' This is, of course, bullshit – a woman can always spot an oyster floating in her drink (especially if you have left on the shell).

A penis

Happiness

In bars and nightclubs all over Britain, so much crap is pouring from the mouths of priapic men into the ears of intoxicated females every weekend. And crap, of course, being an excellent fertilizer, often serves its function, leading to further generations of Britons who will go on to spread their seed in exactly the same manner. Most French women, of course, would not be seen dead in a British nightclub. You may find one dead in the boot of an illegal minicab outside the club perhaps, but not in the club itself.

Here are some of the lines that British men perpetually assure one another will lead to instant sex:

'Is that a ladder in your tights or a stairway to heaven?'

It's a risky game to approach a woman with this amount of religious inference – it is unlikely that a woman in such an establishment is in any way religious herself, given that most religious laws discourage excessive drinking, practising anything other than worship during the weekend and displaying 85 percent of one's tits. Not only this, you are also suggesting a certain level of low personal maintenance. If a girl's clothing on a night out is imperfect, the last thing she requires is a man making this instantly obvious to her while also attempting to get to the other side of those garments. If you must mention this, at least suggest a decent tailor – try to assist the girl using something other than your penis.

'Did it hurt when you fell from heaven?'

Again, a little Jesusy as an approach. Worse, in fact than the previous ladder-based line, as this suggests more than a little bruising or denting on her person. Given such a fall, I think her tights would be the least of her worries. Really though, a British man should avoid any line suggesting physical pain, as he will no doubt by this stage be already invading the woman's personal space with an air of intent and a drunken stare. Certain women, of course, are into this kind of thing, but the chances are they will be found in a more niche establishment, usually with a whip in one hand and a man's balls in the other.

'Nice legs – when do they open?'

A kind of retail-based line here, suggesting a monetary transaction, the implications of which I should not need to cover in great detail. If I do, and you are reading this page for advice, you should simply skip this section and head to Soho with a wallet full of money and a pocket full of condoms made by a reputable manufacturer.

Scooping and throwing an ice cube from a drink: 'Well, now we've broken the ice ...'

I find it hard to believe this has ever led to anything other than ejection from the premises. A woman, when ordering a cocktail, may choose vodka, grenadine, possibly Cointreau (unlikely in a British nightclub), but never 'hand'. Given the level of hygiene in most British establishments' toilets, this is not so much a romance technique, but more an attempt at low-level poisoning. By the time a man is ready to blurt out his woeful play-on-words in this situation, he will no doubt have been slapped and deserted or left dripping in cocktail, spit and regret.

'That dress would look great lying on my bedroom floor.'

A rare allusion by a British man to wild abandon in the bedroom. In truth, both parties know that one of two things will occur:

1. The man will be so uptight and fastidious that he will feel compelled to hang the dress in a wardrobe or, at the very least, on a hanger or fold it neatly and put it in a drawer, rather than leave it on the floor.
2. The man will be so utterly bewildered by the actual success of this chat-up line, against all odds, that his excitement will lead to his own part in the lovemaking coming to an abrupt end before the dress is even fully removed, leading to apologies, possible tears and his paying of a dry-cleaning bill.

'Here's 10p. Call your mother and tell her you won't be home tonight.'

Cheap in more than one way, this line of course implies that the recipient of such advice cannot afford a mobile phone. If indeed this is the case, it is also a highly risky venture, as it not only suggests you do not trust her with your own phone, but sets up an unnecessary obstacle for her – having to leave the club in order to find a public phone (not an easy task in modern times), risking having to queue again for the club and re-entering only to discover you have invested another 10p on another witless and gullible female.

'If I were to rearrange the alphabet I would put "U" and "I" together ...'

If I were a woman approached with this particular gem of wisdom I am sure my first reaction would be: 'who has given this man the authority to make such a linguistic manoeuvre?' The chances of this man being able to perform even basic sexual moves are slim enough, let alone be allowed to make permanent changes to the foundations of an entire set of languages.

'I am a thief and I am here to steal your heart.'

Any woman who has not already departed after the fourth word of this particular attempt deserves all she gets, even a man so socially bereft that he must resort to such lines in the first place.

So, there you go. Men, I hope you have learned something from this. Women also.

The fact that you use the term 'casual sex' in Britain for a one-night sex session should give some indication of the levels of passion brought to the bedroom by the average British male.

Be sensible. Choose French.

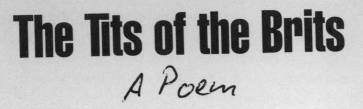

The Tits of the Brits

A Poem

British women have the largest breasts of Europe. It has been suggested (by me) that this is due to their desire to expand out of their confinement, to actually experience some sunshine for once. British men have an unquenchable desire for oversized breasts and most cannot even turn the front page of a newspaper without being comforted by them directly afterwards.

THE TITS OF THE BRITS
                    Are the biggest and best
        Breasts
                    In Europe, they say
But who are they to say?
            And is biggest best
                            Anyway?

When they stay out to play in a man's randy hands
        Will they stand to attention, without intervention?

    And that's not to mention the standard of man
You'll encounter when touting your mountainous Peaks;
        Men who d r o o l like a fool
And truly lose all cool as they   stare   all the while
                    At the vertical smile
            Of a   gleaming,   heaving   cleavage.

When men end their frenzied endeavours with haste,
  ignoring your face
     The fun's up and although the
             D-cup runneth over

The owner's alone, now the boner has gone.

  The petite titty sits pretty when tipped up,
    It's tip-top when on top,
    The sleek subtle peaks within reach,
     Each a pink pointy peach.

Pity the big titty
    Who claims superiority
When, in later years, gravity interferes
  So instead of two spheres
    They will smother your ears
      As you sleep in your bed

Dreaming instead
    You were blessed
  With a chest
     Which may not have impressed
       The testosteroned drones

Who won't rest in their quest
  To squeeze handfuls of flesh,
    While the smartest attest
     That biggest
       Is not
     Best.

The Tits of the Brits

The Class System

Britain is a confused nation, having been raped, pillaged and, worse, Americanized. If certain newspapers are to be believed, the country is now also overrun by immigrants, who are running around and biting the heads off swans. The most popular way for the citizens of Britain to find some identity is via the class system, with which they are obsessed.

Upper class

Whether they admit it or not, many Britons would give anything to be part of the upper class, who are defined by having the largest cars, the most equine laughs and the smallest gene pool.

Most of the upper class have been educated at a public school, to which the general public are not allowed to send their children. Royals and nobility are often sent to

Full upper class plumage

these schools, about which I have heard various rumours. If true, this would certainly explain their tense and awkward walking style, not to mention their manner of speaking as though in extreme rectal discomfort.

A good way of attracting a passing upper-class Briton is with a hat – the larger the better. The upper classes reach a state of near-sexual fervour over certain types of hat and even hold upper-class social functions where the event itself is clearly second to the hats on display.

The upper classes will avoid using consonants wherever possible and make up their own vowels to prove that they are better than everyone else.

Upper-class hobbies include: anything involving horses or shooting, buying properties in the South of France – pushing up house prices to ridiculous levels and then wondering why such local animosity is aimed their way.
Typical upper-class names include: Jocasta, Quentin and Ryvita.

Middle class

The category in which one will find most Britons, as is to be expected in a nation where most things are distinctly average. Fortunately, they are the easiest to understand conversationally. However, many are uneasy of finding themselves in this midway category and so either:

- Act as though they are more upper class, by buying a certain kind of car, house or partner.
- Act as though they are more lower class, for 'street credibility', by making movies where every character speaks in 'Cockney', then marrying the American singer Madonna.

The main resentment of the middle classes is that, unlike those of the upper class, they must work to earn money. Members of the upper-middle class usually ensure they gain employment that will still allow them to subjugate citizens of lower rank, such as a bank manager or army officer. Middle management is, of course, where many of the lower-middle class will find themselves within a company's structure, performing the tasks that the upper management do not wish to do themselves and forever being reminded that they attended the 'wrong' school.

Many middle-class teenagers will go on a 'gap year' in between leaving school and studying a degree that they will soon forget. The gaining of knowledge is often less important to young British people than going overseas to behave like barbaric thugs in Southeast Asia, build up their levels of smugness in India or irritate the shit out of a tribe in Botswana.

Nowadays middle-class parents are giving their children previously antiquated British names such as Alfred, Edith and Neville so that they will 'grow into them' by the time they are 65.

If there is one thing the average white middle-class Briton fears more than running out of tea, it is being inadvertently racist. Although seemingly part of an integrated society, they will have only a few dark-skinned friends. This, of course, is handy when using the defensive phrase 'some of my best friends are black/Asian/slightly foreign' if they fear a racial faux pas has been made. Of course, the middle classes love being 'ironically racist', when amongst an all-white group of friends, as 'actual' racism is seen as something performed by the lower classes, who are often, in fact, more integrated than them.

Most of England's middle classes are stored in Surrey.

Middle-class hobbies include: snowboarding, gossip
and collecting 'Bags For Life'.
Middle-class names include: Nick, John, Steve and Chris.

Lower class*

My words towards this class of person may seem unduly harsh, but do not be concerned, it is very unlikely that any of them will be reading this. Certainly not by this stage, having previously encountered a plethora of elongated words in antecedent chapters. Now that most manual work is done by machines, unemployment is high among Britain's lower class, once ironically named the 'working' class (the opposite being the 'upper' or 'non-working' class). Many collect government benefits each week, which encourage them to enter The National Lottery, breed deadly dogs and develop new swear words.

Council estates are the most common places to observe the lower classes, which have their own internal class system and are seemingly ruled by those with the most tattoos or the least teeth.

---

* It is occasionally difficult on first sight to distinguish the lower from the upper classes, due to certain shared traits – a penchant for Burberry clothing, eyes often a little too close together and a strong disregard for certain animals, while remaining unusually close to others.

The positive benefits of there being less work available is that many of the lower classes now have more time to appear on daytime television shows and 'reality TV' for the benefit of making the middle classes feel better about themselves.

One of these has just urinated in a lift

In turn the lower classes like nothing better than to look down on celebrities, especially when photographed from a bad angle or looking slightly fat.

Around 2,000 magazines are available in Britain focusing on celebrity 'scandals', aimed at the lower classes and costing on average 12p. The middle classes buy them en masse as well, to read 'ironically'.

In France our celebrities are chosen on merit and talent, in Britain the entry grades for super-star status appear to be marrying a footballer (regardless of his attitude regarding fists and women), attending not just the right party, but *every single party*, and being generally loathsome. It is lucky that you have Stephen Fry, who is raising the average levels for British celebrities.

Children of the British lower-lower classes are terrifying. Some of them are known as 'hoodies' due to their attire – usually a cap and a hooded top. The British also use the term 'hood' for the covering of a gentleman's penis. And, like the penis, hoodies are unpredictable, the perfect carriers of disease and unwelcome in most shopping centres. In any British town one is never more than 10 metres away from a lower-class child. A harrowing statistic.

Lower-class hobbies include: Scratchcards, fighting and alcoholism.
Lower-class names include: Shaz, Mick, Nev, Gav, Jaz and Divot.

TOP 10
Overheard Upper-Class Conversations

1. 'So, WHICH servant was Malcolm fucking?'

2. 'No, Rwanda, you can't have a pony until you're 12. You know that.'

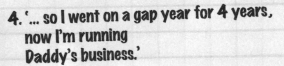

3. '... No, they didn't press any charges – Simeon's father's a High Court Judge. And on the board of the RSPCA, ironically.'

4. '... so I went on a gap year for 4 years, now I'm running Daddy's business.'

5. 'Seriously Toby, nothing says, "Who's top of the food chain?" like a fox with its guts ripped out by a dog, before being trampled to death by a man on a horse. You must come with us sometime.'

6. 'I know a girl in Bali who'll do that, and you don't even have to help her clean up afterwards.'

7. 'I mean, the only "Big Issue" as far as I'm concerned is why we don't just dump them all on an island somewhere.'

8. '... so the most humane thing was to have her put down. On the plus side I got my inheritance quicker.'

9. 'Well they DO, don't they? How can it be "racist" when they actually DO? I met some once and they definitely did.'

10. 'Let's hire a limo, get utterly wankered and shout at people.'

TOP 10
Overheard Lower-Class Conversations

1. 'I've had to get her smaller earrings – she kept getting her dummy caught in them.'

2. 'The thing is, yeah, I'm not being funny, but that's what I'm talking about, innit, do you know what I mean?'

3. 'No, seriously, she still got pregnant and I only fingered her. The kid pops out, and it's not even the right colour.'

4. 'Don't be a dick Gary, that don't count. Bacardi Breezers ain't got real fruit in them.'

5. 'Check out my dog, it's already killed three ducks and shit in a bus.'

6. 'Of course it's not fake Terry – the logo's MEANT to be upside down innit?'

7. 'I'm England 'til I die! England 'til I die! Oh come on England, you're fucking shit!'

8. 'I couldn't get off the couch for two days. That's how you know it's good shit.'

9. 'Nah, of course she ain't suspicious. I just told her we're going on it as part of the audience. Got to find out who the real dad is somehow.'

10. 'Let's hire a limo, get utterly wankered and shout at people.'

The Monarchy

Why Do You Think We Got Rid of Ours?

Many British families, I am told, visit France solely to drag their sticky, gap-toothed spawn to the abomination that is Disneyland Paris. I say, why bother? If you wish your children to witness a creature with an oversized head waddling around speaking unintelligibly while neglecting to wear trousers, you can save some Euros by visiting Windsor Castle, Buckingham Palace or Balmoral.

If you fear you would be missing out on a 'European experience' don't worry – this inexplicably popular family of inbreds have seen more European entrants than the equally inexplicable Eurovision Song Contest. It is ironic that the kind of Brit who claims to hate the Germans with a passion will often fervently support the Royal Family with the same passion.*

---

* An alternative title to this chapter was to be 'No Saxe-Coburg-Gotha Please, We're British'.

Democracy

Few Britons see the irony of sending British troops out to instil *democracy* into countries, when those troops have come from a land whose head of state they are not allowed to vote for.

In 1992, when news of the fire at Windsor Castle reached France, a part of me hoped that the British people had finally had enough and done the honourable thing by their country. However, this was a little too much to hope for, evidently. A British storming of a castle would no doubt involve a tutting mob approaching with clipboards and angry letters, having packed a picnic in case the weather happens to be sunny. When 2 million of your people march against an illegal war and it still occurs, surely a nation has to question the value of any of its leaders, elected or otherwise.

All I am saying is, two centuries ago, the French did a pretty good job of making a point, at a time when the economy was in trouble, money had been squandered on American affairs and the common man was made to feel impotent by the rulers of his country.

Come on Britain, do you really believe one family to be worth 35 million pounds of your money each year? Take a step out of the past. Tourists would still buy the tea towels.

Queen Victoria

Britain's longest-reigning monarch is responsible for the longest-held British traits – namely sexual repression, not being amused, an obsession with new technology and believing that Britain owns everything. Well, I suppose I too would be reticent in discussing sex if I were married to my own cousin. And yet her offspring pervaded Europe, somehow convincing the world that they were entitled to more glittery things than anyone else.

The Queen

Very much like the British rock band Queen: overrated, bigger in the 80s and still going despite the most popular member of her group being dead. It is not known whether Ben Elton is writing a musical about her, but it

Just spotted a poor person?

would be no surprise. The profile view of her face on coins, curiously similar to the profile of other European royals, is for the British a symbol of supposedly being too good for the Euro.

The Queen is said to be good for British tourism and there is a wonderful irony that European tourists coming to see 'Her Majesty' and her various palaces will be royally ripped off when having to exchange their currency to do so.

The Queen's main duties involve opening a door once a year to let the Parliament in, speaking on television for seven minutes every Christmas and having two birthdays. Her 'Official Birthday' in June, two months after the actual day of her birth, is held so that celebrations can take place 'with better weather'. Of all the excuses for having a second birthday, this is perhaps the least believable – what cause does any Briton have to believe that one month will be any more reliable than any other?

The Queen Mother

This should, of course, be 'The Queen's Mother' but the Royals are so stuck-up they believe they can defy grammar. This woman lived to be 101 years old. The key to living this long, then, would appear to be: 'waving' as a main occupation and a general diet of gin, Dubonnet and swans. This woman had 83 full-time staff, for which the public seemed happy to pay with their taxes, while still wondering why their local roads had holes in them and their schools and hospitals were below standard.

Prince Philip

In my opinion, the sole reason for keeping the British monarchy. His outdated, misjudged comments are just as enjoyable as his grovelling attempts to apologize for them afterwards.

The man is a walking time-bomb of anachronistic commentary and will always have my full attention when featured on news stories while making international visits. He has the air of a man who is simply feeling lucky to be in such a position in the first place (as if this singles him out from any member of the Royal Family), while also able to get away with such things, as he is not, and never will be, King. Although he is, like his wife the Queen, a great-great-grandchild of Queen Victoria, there are reasons why he is not allowed to be King, although they are so dull and outdated that nobody can bring themselves to elaborate on them.

Just spotted an ethnic?

Prince Charles

In a move to avoid further alienation of the British public by the British Royal Family, Charles chose his mother's surname of 'Windsor' over the more unpalatable 'Schleswig-Holstein-Sonderburg-Glücksburg'. And, indeed, what could be more British than avoiding anything with an *umlaut*?

Demonstrating his chances of being King

To justify his existence, Charles travels the world warning people of the effects of global warming, with his ears warning people of the effects of interbreeding. The fact that Charles makes these environmental visits in a private jet should not alter your judgment of his efforts. Do not forget we are speaking of a country that is used to being constantly lectured by the Irish pop star Bono about altruism and environmental concerns, while he deposits his earnings in a Dutch account to avoid tax and is happy to buy a first-class aeroplane flight for a hat.

Faux-pas-on-legs junior

Princess Diana

Does it not say something that the most popular royal of modern times in Britain has been a woman who, according to their own rules, was not technically a royal at all?

An investigation into the Spencer family reveals no German lineage whatsoever, which must have been a disappointment to Charles' parents, as must her misplaced humility that hinders the portrayal of royals as superior beings. Eventually, Diana chose happiness over Wales and so rejected this strange family from her life. But, while visiting Paris in 1997, Diana was killed, a Parisian welcome even worse than is usually given to visiting Britons in that city. It was decided that the most fitting tribute to Diana would be a malfunctioning fountain in a London park, constructed perhaps with the British rail service in mind, as its failure was in fact attributed to a 'rogue leaf'.

Prince William

The human face of the British Royals – to be expected when you let an outsider into your gene pool. Over the years William has proved himself to be disappointingly normal and devoid of controversy, discounting the use of a helicopter to impress a girl. But given that part of his title is 'Royal Knight Companion of the Most Noble Order of the Garter' it is perhaps only a matter of time before a story of cross-dressing emerges in the news. Not that this would be considered unusual by most of the British public.

Prince Harry

Another one to watch whenever featured on news reports, whether dressing as a member of The Third Reich or smoking marijuana, there are constant rumours that Harry, whose name is actually 'Henry' is in fact an illegitimate child of Diana.

Surely the Nazi uniform incident, along with various race-based gaffes, should assure the public that he is very certainly descended from Prince Philip?

Like his father, there appears to be in him a certain frustration that he will never be King, with the added frustration that he will always be ginger. I still like to believe that he is attempting to bring down the royals from the inside. Especially as he is licensed to drive a tank.

The Latest Royal Wedding

The world's media ensured we could not avoid the sight of Prince William bonding Kate Middleton to his degenerate family, and the ghoulish parade of hats, jewellery and overbites was of course used as an enormous PR exercise by Britain's inexplicably numerous royalists to boost the flagging reputation of these anachronistic dinosaurs, painting them as relevant and progressive. No doubt the government are hoping that this will keep up enough positive momentum among the British to gloss over the inevitable crushing disappointment of Britain's management of the Olympics.

ASK MARCEL

1

Dear Marcel, I have been with the same woman for four years, and we have been living together for two of those years. We both work from home, and so are rarely apart. At first I thought this would be a positive thing but I feel we're rapidly growing tired of each others' company. Can you recommend anything? – **Simon Samuels, Runcorn**

Marcel Says: Four years? Already this sounds too clingy for me. Me, I tend to move on. But, if you insist on pursuing this tiresome monogamous charade, to keep alive the spark for you, I would recommend leaving small notes around the house for your woman. Three word notes are the best – a different word hidden in a different room of the house, and the best three words one can leave are 'WILL', 'YOU' and 'ME'. She will be searching for the fourth word for days. This gives you time for your own leisure activities and will keep the spark alive for you.

Alternatively, why not try hiding? Women, they enjoy a game, and I am told 'hide-and-seek' is a popular British game, especially for those avoiding the paying of tax, or the murder of train drivers. Why not begin with some simple hiding – in the cupboard with some flowers or wine – and then progress to more advanced hiding, for example, for several weeks at the house of another woman? A sister of hers, perhaps. If eventually she does find you, you can reward her efforts with some light sex, if you have the strength. Hiding has been an admirable trait in a man since times of prehistory. It has ensured his survival. Some men are able to hide for decades. See how long you can manage.

Marcel

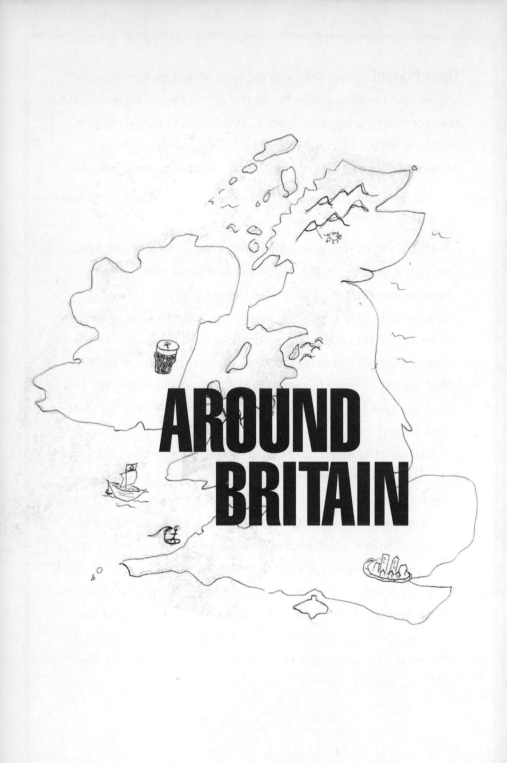

AROUND BRITAIN

'If the UNITED Kingdom and GREAT Britain surprise you with their lack of UNITY and GREATness, wait until you see Weston-SUPER-Mare.'

England

Ah, *la perfide Albion*! For a country of such diminutive stature, England really does seem to have done an incredible job, over the years, of angering most countries of the world. Even their neighbour, Wales, charges them money to visit. And whenever England are playing an international sporting contest against France, we know who Scotland, Wales and Ireland* will be cheering for.

English arrogance

In many ways, England is like a bully of the school playground who may have prematurely stopped growing, but still insists that everyone calls him 'sir'. He insists also that everyone should speak his own language (just a mix of others' languages, but do not tell him this). Everyone else would happily gather together and take him on, were it not for his larger American cousin, who has all the latest catapults (except for the ones he sold to the boys from the rough school down the road). He even carries his own type of money, as he believes himself to be better than everyone on the other side of the river, despite having very little evidence of this. However, a lot of his 'best mates' have gone their individual ways, sick of being told what to do. His self-loathing over this manifests itself in defensive proclamations, such as not wanting any more friends as his house is now 'full'.

Government

England is governed by a London-based Parliament, currently in a coalition of two wildly differing parties, the Conservatives (or 'Tories'),

---

* Perhaps not the latter any more, after the fracas over Thierry Henry. If I have to hear about this one more time from an Irishman, I shall punch them in the face and then claim that in fact it was a case of 'face-to-hand.'

most of whom were privately-educated and are led by a wealthy graduate of 'Oxbridge', and the Liberal Democrats (or 'Lucky Bastards'), most of whom were privately-educated and led by a wealthy graduate of 'Oxbridge'. And, fortunately, the public knows they have a governing body they can trust – 76 percent of the 'Cabinet' (senior members of the Government elected by the Prime Minister) are millionaires, so they know they are in reliable hands.

In October 2010, the year after the revelation of Members of Parliament 'borrowing' money from the general public for helipads, moats and pornography, the government's millionaire chancellor (who once claimed £440 in expenses for a taxi to his home) made cuts resulting in 490,000 British job losses. The British were furious, tutting much, much louder than usual and raising their eyebrows up and down very strongly indeed.

Saint George

The patron saint of England is Saint George, who was born in Cappadocia, Turkey. A real testament to exaggerated English gossip and rumour, he was said to have killed a dragon. This image resonates with modern Englishmen, who are used to their people entering into mythical battles, such as the 'War on Terror'.

Culture

Culturally, England has the same deluded sense of superiority that it has on the sporting field, but one must simply switch on a television, a radio or an electronic reading device (previously known as a 'book') to see the truth. Once a nation with a proud record of literary heroes – William Wordsworth, George Orwell, D.H. Lawrence – Britain's modern output now seems to cater largely for anybody who is into wizards, teenage vampires or watching celebrities implode. And when it comes to music, although the English could never hope to reach the level of emotion of Jacques Brel, Edith Piaf or Serge Gainsbourg, at least they would give it a try.

Bloody idiots

These days, every time I have attempted to discover something I would define as music on an English radio station, my ears have instead been battered by what I believe the Americans describe as 'R and B' – supposedly 'Rhythm and Blues' – but containing neither of these elements. It is a hugely popular form of music all over Britain for men with no self-control and women with no self-respect. Horrific.

The North–South divide

It is no great surprise that there is some animosity between the north and the south English. It is the way of the world to detest one's neighbouring country, but the English have to be even more localized about this.

In France, most of us prefer simply to direct our negative emotions towards Parisians. In England, the north English see themselves as more tough, living in a greyer part of the country (weather *and* surroundings).

Welcome to the high street

The south English think of themselves simply as better. Not, as one might expect, due to their proximity to France, but instead largely due to a lack of industrial eyesores, racial unrest and Northerners. While I have noticed slight differences between the two parties during my time here, both seem united in their misplaced pride for their own area.

There is also a language divide between the North and the South, with those from the North saying 'nowt' instead of 'nothing', 'ta' instead of 'thanks', and 'yawha?' instead of 'I'm sorry, could you repeat that please?'. There are also some colourful Northern phrases, such as 'haway pet', 'ahh kid' and 'death ta pooftas'.

Don't be misled...

For every positive aspect of a place, an equally negative one soon cancels it out. For example, Cornwall may have more picturesque sights than the locals can count on their superfluous fingers, but walk into the wrong pub with the wrong clothing, sexuality or skin tone, and you may end up like a local apple – pulped, put in a barrel or 'scrumped'. I still have no real

England

idea what this means, nor do I wish to. Kent is known as 'The Garden of England' but of course, like in any garden, among the plants, fruits and wildlife, one will also find many a shit, some colourful views and the occasional pervert.

England has a number of towns designed to trick, such as Southport, which is in the north, Eastbourne in the south and Weston-super-Mare, which is anything but super.*

Customer service

The Emperor Napoleon described Britain as a 'nation of shopkeepers'. What he failed to mention is the ineptitude with which these shops are kept. I just do not believe the phrase 'how can I help you?' should be rhetorical. Most employees of retail outlets in England seem to have been hired for their prowess in staring contests, rather than any actual knowledge about the products in stock.

Telephone exchanges are an equally sorrowful affair too, when attempting to deal with any British service. The robotic voice one is greeted with maximizes frustration and minimizes the possibility of vocal vengeance when reporting something wrong with a product – an all-too-frequent occurrence. And if ever anyone does find themselves speaking to an actual human, in a post-colonial manoeuvre that is almost to be applauded in its audacity, it is 96 percent likely that the call has been re-routed to India, where a worker is paid a minimal amount to receive one's words of fury concerning a substandard British service.

A great English day out

For a country that seems to believe it invented time†, England is often tragically in the past. Every year baying English mobs will gather at

---

* I am aware that this title, of course, is derived from the Latin but please allow me to gloss over this so as to denigrate Weston-super-Mare, a terrifyingly Neandarthal town.

† Not an entirely negative thing – it is always good to see '+1' written next to France when compared to England, in time-related cases or otherwise.

various times and locations to see, among other things:

- Toothless old people creating torturous expressions through a horse's collar.

- Unskilled locals throwing themselves from a pier into the sea wearing rudimentary 'flying' apparatus.

- Men chasing an uncatchable cheese down a steep hill, where ambulances await to tend to their broken bones.

Aspiration: a duck. Reality: a dick

And, if an English man's fertility is ever questioned, he can simply steer you to any English field in May, where men in floral hats waving sticks and handkerchiefs at one another can be seen, accompanied by the sound of jangling bells attached to their big white manly socks.

A great English night out

For a truly authentic English experience, why not head to any town centre for a tea or coffee in an American chain coffee house, followed by a top meal in any of the Thai, Indian or Chinese restaurants and a trip to the nearest multiplex cinema or bowling alley? If you are still hungry after all this your main option is a Turkish kebab.

England 45

Scotland

Wild, ragged and windy, the Scottish are perhaps the toughest people of all the Britons, certainly when it comes to deciphering their hastily-spoken and often consonant-free sentences. They inherited their fiery hair from the Vikings. Appropriately, their flame-haired women often have fiery tempers too, as I discovered during my time performing at the Edinburgh Festival. I should have known, when removing the knickers, that red means 'danger'.

The Scottish–French alliance

Perhaps the most admirable trait of the Scottish is the lengths they will often go to to distance themselves from the English. France has always recognized and appreciated this, especially given that the poor Scottish do not even have a body of water to separate themselves from these people, although it is worth noting that a large wall still remains in position, long since its intended purpose has passed, and nobody has thought to take it down.

The Scottish have assisted France many times over the centuries (including Jeanne d'Arc's great battles against the megalomaniac English) and have heeded our expert advice when it comes to many things, including building castles, the legal system and thinking.

Despite so many factors that seem to scream 'GET THE FUCK OUT OF OUR LAND' – a prickly floral emblem, an often impenetrable accent, a national instrument sounding like a newly-castrated goat, skin so pale it reflects sunlight and a monster in a lake – the Scottish are a remarkably welcoming race.

The kilt

The national dress, or should I say, the national skirt, may appear at first quite an anomaly for such a tough nation, but do not let this fool you.

Skirts are worn by two types of men:

1. Those who believe they were born with the wrong genitalia.
2. Those who are happy to display their genitalia within seconds of a strong gust of wind or at the request of an inquisitive female – rendering another person's mockery of such attire a particularly foolish move.

The Scottish man mainly falls into category number 2, and it should be noted by anyone wishing to test my theory that traditional attire also includes a knife carried in the sock.

In Scotland one is only ever one gust away from a penis

Certain Scottish women also opt for this thick, plaited skirt-and-sock combination. Such women are, by and large, bi and large.

Culinary delights

Like any nation of culture, the Scottish enjoy eating every part of an animal. However, rather than savour each part individually, instead they gather it all together in a stomach – nature's Tupperware. The 'haggis' is depicted sometimes as a creature in its own right, especially in books for children. Bizarre, given what a ghoulish image this is – a kind of meat zombie galloping across the land.

A true Scot will toughen himself up not only externally, but internally too, by testing his inner organs on a daily basis. It is unknown from where the Scottish obsession with deep-frying anything previously edible arises –

perhaps as a homage to the once-popular pastime of frying suspected witches. It is no wonder the women of Scotland are so tough.

Perhaps it is another way to outdo and distance themselves from the English, who instead choose to boil all their food wherever possible.

But, in this land where fruit is considered a delicacy, no food seems off limits for deep-frying and consuming. During my time there, I witnessed not only deep-fried pizza, but also deep-fried ice cream (which I did not believe was even physically possible until I witnessed it) and the deep-fried Mars bar. I was assured by a Scottish acquaintance that the latter is in fact a joke food to sell to Americans, which of course is a move to be admired. I tried to verify this a week later, but alas my acquaintance had since died of heart disease.

Saint Andrew

Their patron saint is Saint Andrew, one of the disciples of Jesus Christ – the Scottish love myths and folklore. In fact, the thistle is Scotland's emblem due to the tale of some Scottish men being awoken in a field by some sneaky invading Vikings, who stood on thistles and let out loud wails. Surely this also explains the bagpipes as a national 'musical' instrument.

The Highlands

Go further North, to the Highlands and the isles of Scotland, and one can truly breathe in fresh air. At times, I am assured, one can also see the Northern Lights, although this could be the brain playing tricks as it reaches the advanced stages of refrigeration.

It is possible that the Vikings were not actually that keen on raping villagers or setting fire to buildings, but merely did both as a way of remaining warm.

Scottish philosophy

With a climate so discordant, and centuries of irritation from the English, it is certainly a country that lends itself to philosophy, producing notable thinkers, most of whom studied this noble art, of course, in France. David Hume, who produced works too complex to be appreciated by the English at the time, was a wonderful exponent of the study of human nature. 'Beauty in things exists,' he said, 'in the mind which contemplates them.' And indeed, one can see this theory being practised every weekend in Scottish cities, as thirsty Scots fill themselves with outrageous quantities of strong liquor to allow their minds to extend the parameters of 'beauty'.

A fighting spirit

Bravery is also a characteristic attributed to the Scottish and in 2007 a man from Glasgow set out to affirm this by demonstrating that the Scottish are not afraid to kick a terrorist, even when that terrorist is on fire, having driven a burning car into Glasgow Airport.

There are many accounts of the Scottish and their brave battles for independence over the English. You can also watch a film about this starring an Australian American, which, I imagine has rewritten history to depict the USA playing an important part in Scotland's independence, despite not being invented for another 500 years.

One needs a 'brave heart' to eat so much deep-fried food

To balance out their highly colourful history, the Scottish have created Aberdeen, a city entirely devoid of colour.

Ireland

With the body of a republic and the head of a United Kingdom annex, Ireland is a divided country in many ways, but at least they know what to do with a vegetable. Northern Ireland is not part of Great Britain, but is part of the United Kingdom, despite being far from united, ever since a fat English king decided to change religion to get rid of a wife.

A warm welcome

If you have previously been in England, what a joy it is to arrive in Ireland, where a smile from a local doesn't render one instantly suspicious, and if people are in a hurry it is just to get to the next music festival. America has not yet got its fat hands on most of the shops, which sell plentiful fresh produce and deep-fat fryers seem in a minority. Less reliance on the potato would be welcomed, but then history has taught them this all too well.

Ireland has seen some tough times, but its people continue to smile and laugh their way through life, which could in part be due to their love of alcohol. A thirsty nation, there are moments while visiting Ireland when one is eyed with suspicion without a drink in hand. After all, there is no excuse when it is so plentifully available.

Irish folklore

Every part of Britain has a mythical element attached to it – for the Scottish, the Loch Ness Monster, for the Welsh, the dragon and for the English, manners. And Ireland is no different, supposedly home to the 'leprechaun', found in folklore, tourist shops and gullible Americans' heads. Again, alcohol may play a part here – the excuse of returning home late due to following a little ginger-bearded man towards the end of a rainbow sounds to me like a tale invented after the eighth whisky.

Ireland has managed to retain its beauty and, unlike England, avoid being trampled by motorways. Its symbol is the delicate shamrock plant, said to represent the Biblical concept of the Holy Trinity of Father, Son and Holy Spirit, very important to the Irish. A shamrock with four leaves is said to be extremely lucky, but if we are sticking with the metaphor, surely this means the Devil has made an appearance? I doubt this theory is enough to alter the folklore now, but perhaps worth considering ...

Culture

With a fairer political system than the UK, a better standard of life and a stylish three-colour flag design, the Republic is a progressive nation and it is easy to understand why many in the North are keen to split from the governance of the UK. Ireland has been ably assisting the culture of the UK over the years, with characters such as Oscar Wilde, Samuel Beckett, James Joyce and George Bernard Shaw. The British film industry has repaid them by casting the Irish as feckless drunks, toothless idiots or violent gypsies.

St Patrick's Day

The national day of the Irish, St Patrick's Day, occurs on 17 March, when the English pay a bit of attention to the Irish for once, as they have given them yet another excuse to drink for Jesus and wear oversized hats. Saint Patrick is said to have rid Ireland of all of its snakes. It is questionable that there ever *were* snakes in Ireland, but in a country so willing to ardently believe every word of the Bible, it is unlikely that this is ever debated.

Wales

Ah, Wales, the part of Britain resembling the head of a pig – something once commonly passed around in English aristocratic society ... much like Wales itself.

The language

The Welsh truly love their consonants – deceptive in a country which seems, like France, to enjoy its vowels so much that it sometimes gives them a little hat. When it comes to their name, even one vowel is too much for the Welsh, who are known in their own language as the 'Cymry' – a name with no vowels at all.

The origins of this vowel-avoidance are unclear – perhaps a mishearing of the word 'Vikings' as 'vowel kings' amidst all the looting, raping and pillaging – but whatever the reason, a glance at the names of their towns is another indication of this bizarre passion for consonants. The best example is *Llanfairpwllgwyngyllgogerychwyrndrobwllllantysiliogogogoch* in Anglesey. This is said to mean 'The church of St Mary in the hollow of white hazel trees near the rapid whirlpool by St Tysilio's of the red cave'. Yet, surely since the invention of the map, such specific directions within a place name are more than a little unnecessary?

I have not visited this town (although I at least know exactly *where* to find it, should I decide to), so I cannot confirm whether or not they have had to breed unusually broad and flat townspeople in order for them to wear the t-shirts or caps promoting their town.

LLANFAIRPWLLGWYNGYLLGOGERYCHWYRNDROBWLLLLANTYSILIOGOGOGOCH

Llan-vire-pooll-guin-gill-go-ger-u-queern-drob-ooll-llandus-ilio-gogo-goch

Despite first appearances, the Welsh are a fairly cultured nation, true to their traditions. As soon as one enters Wales, signs are written in English, with a proud Welsh translation beneath.

The importance of the task of translation being completed by an actual *Welsh* man was highlighted in 2008, after the appearance of a large sign in Swansea reading 'No entry for heavy goods vehicles. Residential site only', with the Welsh translation beneath written as 'Nid wyf yn y swyddfa ar hyn o bryd. Anfonwch unrhyw waith I'w gyfieithu'. This translates as 'I am not in the office at the moment. Send any work to be translated.'

The flag

Not content with having Britain's most difficult language, Wales is also insistent on having the most difficult flag. Instead of going for the simple 'lines and colours' format, they have included an entire dragon. One would think that, through practising the drawing of this, Welsh children would become Britain's best artists, but there is little evidence of this, perhaps because they spent *too* long drawing dragons. And if the child is also educated in *Llanfairpwllgwyngyllgogerychwyrndrobwllllantysiliogogogoch*, once their writing and drawing classes are over, I cannot imagine they have much time left for anything else at all.

Saint David

Unlike the English, the Welsh have chosen as their patron saint a man actually born in their country. Supposedly encouraging his men to wear leeks in their hats during battle, he is responsible for the Welsh people being associated with this pleasant vegetable, which they often use in their cuisine and which is criminally overlooked by the English.

Colonies

The Welsh, not an enormously ambitious nation when foreign expansion is concerned, have just a few colonies, all in remote Patagonia, seemingly to get as far away from the English as possible.

Britain's Bizarre Locations

When leaving a large town or city in Britain you will notice that the local people become more and more difficult to comprehend, and the names of many rural towns are no different. I have taken no time at all to visit the following places, as I fear that if I stop to light a cigarette the inhabitants will be enchanted by my 'fire-in-a-stick' and attempt to burn me for witchcraft. Of course, in the time it would take for them to rub together two sticks I would have made my escape, but still I have better things to do with my time, such as research these bizarre places of Britain, some of which I truly believe must be prank names.

ALSOP-EN-LE-DALE, Derbyshire; ASHBY-DE-LA-ZOUCH, Leicestershire; BURTON-LE-COGGLES, Lincolnshire

Yes, I see what is happening here. A pitiful attempt by the English to retain some Norman stature. 'En-le-Dale', maybe. 'De-la-Zouch', I don't think so. And 'Le-Coggles' ... you are fooling nobody.

AMERICA, Cambridgeshire

Why, why, why? You have given them plenty of your own names, the unoriginal bastards. They do not need the favour returned – they seem to be doing OK trying to run the planet. What is next – 'New New York'?

BALLS CROSS, West Sussex

It is, of course, obvious to simply assume this to be a popular meeting town for those into the practice of wife-sharing, so this is what I shall do.

BARTON IN THE BEANS, Leicestershire

A curious ritual amongst the British is to raise money for charities by bathing in baked beans. I do not know what message this is supposed to deliver, especially if doing so for a hunger-based charity, but I assume that perhaps this town achieved its name by an attempt to submerge it entirely in the foodstuff. Twinned with Barton-Dressed-Like-A-Dick-To-Run-A-Marathon.

BELL END, Worcestershire
Much as I hate to see old traditions die, I believe sometimes one must override such views when one's town, instead of being associated with some old musical practice, becomes instead associated with the end of a man's penis. I imagine the wealthiest man in this town is the signmaker, whose sole job is to replace the town's sign post-theft on an almost daily basis.

BUMMERS HILL, Hertfordshire
See above, although I cannot imagine what quaint British tradition this name has come from. As in French, the term 'gay' has long since ceased to mean 'jolly' or 'happy'. Indeed, in many remote British towns that still contain the word 'gay', or variations on it, their homosexuals are probably the least happy residents of the town.

COCKUP BOTTOM, Cumbria
I would have to observe this with my own eyes before believing it to be a true town. If indeed it does exist, the local signmaker must be the only one to put the signmaker of Bell End into second place.

DANCING DICKS, Essex
I was around Essex on 1 May and did indeed see many of the above. Perhaps this place is the origin of what is said in Britain to be a fertility dance. And judging by the number of single mothers I saw in Essex this does seem to be the case. A dance, a wave of the handkerchief and they are gone.

DEAD COW POINT, Lundy Island
The only activity available in this town, perhaps? Still, a more effective way of making children aware of their own mortality than, for example, 'hopscotch'.

DULL, Pitlochry

Much like 'Muck', 'Hen Poo', 'Raw', 'Rotten Bottom' and 'Wasp's Nest' (all genuine places in the UK), I am deeply suspicious of a place continuing to use such a name, and believe they may be hiding some kind of hidden treasure, such as palatable British cheese or British women who actually enjoy sex. For the opposite, see 'Friendly', below.

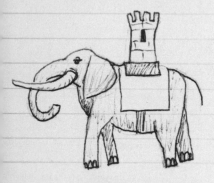

ELEPHANT AND CASTLE, London

This one I have been unfortunate enough to visit and it seems no place for either object. There is truly nothing worth defending with a castle there, and the elephant would last only seconds before being killed and having its legs placed on a skewer in one of the numerous lugubrious kebab houses of the area.

FRENCHBEER, Devonshire

I would hope for this to be a town where every resident is aged either 16 or 64, but alas I fear it is just another example of an English town attempting to appear rather more cultured than it truly is.

FRIENDLY, Yorkshire

This sounds like a trap.

GOOD EASTER, Essex

One can only assume this place to be now entirely unpopulated, after years of its inhabitants tolerating the inevitable greeting from everyone in the entire town around Jesus' deathday weekend with forced grins. It may only be once a year, but for the average human, this is too much to bear. Were I a resident there, I would leave before it all gets too much for one person and a bloody massacre occurs.

GREAT COCKUP, Cumbria

Actually a mountain, rather than a town, but good to know the British have a monument 500 metres high dedicated to their numerous 'cockups'. On a trek up there I would hope to find a shrine to the world's economy, another Bayeux Tapestry and some replica Weapons of Mass Destruction.

LOST, Aberdeenshire

Without a doubt, the worst place to break down (vehicularly or mentally). But spare a thought for any local who decides to move away, who can never truthfully answer the question 'Where are you from?' without fearing the questioner's blood on their hands shortly afterwards. It would be a cruel hand dealt by fate if that person were to marry someone from Good Easter.

MUMBLES, Swansea

Appropriate, I am sure. In Swansea I once spent 17 minutes attempting to identify and order a lunch from a woman whose mouth appeared to open at an angle of no more than 5 degrees.

NETHERTHONG, Yorkshire

Sounding like an instruction for the correct location to wear undergarments, this is of no surprise, given its close proximity to the town Huddersfield, a town whose people seem to have no regard for suitable clothing, even on the coldest of days. If anyone needs clothing advice it is them. A vest is not, and never will be, an acceptable alternative to a coat in winter.

SLATTOCKS, Lancashire

Having been out in towns close by here on weekends, I can only assume this to be a shortened form of 'Slags' Buttocks', as these were the only vaguely redeeming feature in town during my time there.

TWATT, Orkney

A place I have in fact visited, only to find the locals referring to it as 'twart', the warnkers.

WESTON-UNDER-LIZARD, Staffordshire

This village is as likely to be beneath a lizard as Weston-super-Mare is to be described as 'super' by anyone who has ever visited it. Any place trying this hard to sound interesting is probably not.

Transport

The Britons are at their happiest when complaining. This release of frustration is usually to one another rather than to the perpetrator of whatever deed has angered them, which is why the weather is such a popular subject for their infuriation – it is a rare breed of man who chooses to direct his anger at a particular cloud. Of course this does not stop them from directing it towards the Bureau of Meteorology for failing to predict complex global weather patterns that they only partially understand. However, very occasionally the weather of Britain is perfectly adequate, even good, and the frustrations of the nation must be redirected. Providing there is no major sporting event or media scare over immigrants or paedophiles, it is transport that incurs the wrath of the British.

Given the state of Britain's transport, this is a perfectly legitimate use of emotions. In France, our government subsidizes our public transport, including our state-owned railway network, recognizing the importance of people getting around cheaply and efficiently. Britain has opted for the policy of privatization, giving other people the chance to make excuses and rip off the public, while they themselves encourage their citizens to drive less.

Trains

There appears to be a conspiracy to keep people in their own towns, if the price of Britain's trains is anything to go by. With the most expensive rail fares in the whole of Europe *and* the highest petrol prices, it does seem curious.

I recall one occasion when I almost made a visit to Leeds before discovering it would cost £100 on a train for the privilege. This is putting quite a lot of pressure on Leeds – it is saying I will enjoy my trip there every bit as much as two average bottles of wine, a bag of narcotics and a good book, or a bad woman. I am still to go, but I would be highly surprised if this were the case.

A Briton's number 1 method of intimacy with a stranger

With transport this expensive, surely, Marcel, you are saying, this must be the best in the world? One would think so, yes, but in all my travels around this earth, I have never known a train to be afraid of leaves, before coming to Britain. In France, a 'train versus leaf' contest will always see trains as the winners – our wonderful TGV service can reach speeds of 550 kilometres per hour. Visitors to London's Olympics in 2012 will have to undertake quite an Olympic feat themselves to reach the Games if the city's transport remains as it is. Which it probably will.

A train driver will often patronisingly declare at the end of a journey, 'thank you for travelling with us', even if there has been no other option to reach one's destination and the journey has lasted twice its intended duration. It is yet another example of the British trying to appear polite at all times, and surely it cannot be long before one can see 'thank you for using the pavement' signs all over Britain. Occasionally on a train one is lucky enough to be an aural witness to the latter stages of a train driver's mental breakdown, as some garbled lunatic rantings are barked through the speaker system to the confused passengers. It is to be expected, I suppose – it takes a certain kind of man to be immune to being trapped in a metal canister and made to repeat a journey backwards and forwards to the same destination for decades.

Buses

While waiting at a bus stop in Britain, one is advised to carry several items of warm clothing and at least two meals, as the bus times written on the timetables have been invented randomly. For many local bus companies the concept of offering change is yet to be discovered, which may explain the erratic times of arrival, as geriatrics fumble around in purses and pockets at every stop to appease the despotic driver. Most bus drivers in Britain are only ever happy when driving away from a person they have spotted in the mirror running to the bus stop as though running for the final rocket to leave Earth.

Some cities have night buses, which offer the same infrequency and *froideur* of the day bus, but without the daylight. It is here that one truly understands the misanthropy of the bus driver, as anyone placed on one of these shifts, even once in his life, must develop an undying hatred for humanity as a species.

Coaches

Coach trips over longer distances can be a gamble for one's spinal column, sanity and bladder. One can buy a coach trip for as little as £1 and these services contain just the kind of human one would expect. To those complaining all the way through the journey: this five-hour trip has cost you less than that meat pie you are currently grinding into your face.

What did you expect? I would also advise any traveller intending to sit near the toilets for easy access to reconsider this move – the toilet, if it works at all, has generally, it seems, been used as storage for a deceased pet, judging by the odour as soon as one opens the door.

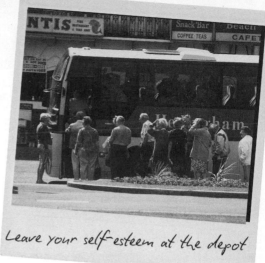

Leave your self-esteem at the depot

Cars

Despite the highest price for fuel in Europe, constant roadworks and major congestion issues in the cities, car travel is still extremely popular in Britain. Many young men are convinced that a shiny new car, or a shiny old car with an extra exhaust pipe fitted and darkened windows, will attract the woman of their dreams, before discovering that their dreams have misled them and that all it will attract are other men attempting to outrun you at traffic lights.

Motorways

Motorways are labelled with 'M' and a number. As far as I can tell, the 'M' not only signifies the word 'motorway' but also 'misery', the number representing the level of misery to be expected from the experience of using it. For evidence of this, compare the M1 and M25 roads. Many British motorways simply follow the path of Roman roads. Roman influence is evident in many British things still, from bribery and corruption among the upper classes, to believing that where a certain set of stars is this week has any influence at all on your life and prospects.

Taxis

With public transport in its current state, the taxi is abundant all over Britain. There is not much I can say about the taxi drivers of Britain – as soon as one announces oneself to be French they are usually silent.

Taxi drivers of London must memorize every one of London's often poorly-signed streets for 'The Knowledge' – a test which also requires them to memorize basic racial generalizations and outdated views about world politics. Many also have an inexplicable fear of travelling to the other side of the River Thames. I say, 'why learn an entire map of the place, and then only choose to operate in one half of it?'

Rank

I have been told that, due to congestion, taxis in the centre of London travel on average at the same speed as the horse and cart did a century ago. At least with the horse one would get less crap and a better attitude.

Aeroplanes

Obsessed with air travel, presumably once again in an attempt to compete with America, Britain has an extraordinary number of airports and an equally large selection of low-budget airlines, ranging from the borderline criminal to the terrifying. When a small can of drink and a sandwich costs more than the flight itself, questions must be asked. To allay the terror of travelling on one of these contraptions, there are things one can do to distract the mind momentarily, such as pretending instead that one is on a flight simulator – the cheap plastic nature of the seating and general structure of the plane renders this relatively easy. And, on the subject of 'easy', on a certain brand of cheap airline, one can play a game to pass the time by attempting to find the steward or stewardess whose unnatural skin colour most closely matches the logo of the air company.

Travel Games

Britain may be small, but never underestimate how long a journey will last, whatever the advertised duration. Delays, line closures and the increasingly popular 'rail replacement service' must all be factored in. Here are just two things one might witness to keep one entertained:

Random acts of misguided kindness

Several times I have had the pleasure to see a young man give up his seat to a pregnant woman, only to discover she is simply morbidly obese. The woman grows angry, the man's face grows red and passengers attempt to hide their smiles amidst palpable awkwardness. In this position I would say, 'Madam, I am doing you a favour. Unless you do something about this, this will continue to happen'.

And to fat persons in jogging costumes on buses one wishes to say, 'Simply to wear the costume will not make you thin. The requisite exercise must also be achieved.' And one could probably say this to their faces – I imagine it is rare that they will chase you. Even if they do, in three minutes they'll be out of breath or they will have spotted a McDonald's.

Train toilet terror

Using a toilet on public transport is like the city of Birmingham – with planning it can be avoided, and it is only marginally preferable to shitting oneself. Certain trains have fitted a bizarre toilet with a curved and slowly retracting door, supposedly to look futuristic, although to most travellers it is more 'tense psychological thriller' than 'science fiction.' Occasionally, one can witness an unfortunate who has failed to master this public 'convenience's' flawed locking system, and can only look on in terror as the door slowly opens at the request of another, horrifyingly and unavoidably revealing their dirty deeds to the entirety of the carriage.

The Seasons

Here is a guide to Britain's seasons. Note that, unlike in France, most public holidays of the British are usually made to occur on the weekend, instead of the more simple option of sticking to the same date each year.* This is so that they have at least one, often two, days where they can attempt to destroy as many brain cells as possible using alcohol, in order to forget the monotony of the job they must return to once the holiday is over.

If you ever see 'Remember: clocks go forward' written on the front of a British newspaper, the publication is not simply trying to explain to the public the nature of time – it is merely informing them that their day has effectively been extended, encouraging bosses to demand even longer working hours, still without an appropriate length of lunch break.

The British often complain about the weather, but one would think they are used to it by now, and they seem to forget that it is because of bad weather that they have not had to learn the language of Spanish since 1588.

* With the exception, of course, of most Jesus-based holidays. 2,000 years on, he still has to be the centre of attention. Grow up Jesus.

Spring

Typified by cool, changeable temperatures, drizzle and occasional sunshine, springtime is a season when the British traditionally jettison any resolutions they have made for the new year and instead fool themselves that they are making a change in their lives by brushing everything in their houses with a duster and clearing away things they do not need into boxes, which are put on top of other boxes.

Parts of Britain actually begin to look OK in the spring, with flowers and trees in bloom and a bountiful supply of fruit and vegetables (if only you knew how to properly treat them in the kitchen). The British will marvel at the new life beginning all around them and then grumble about the 'April showers,' which are in fact keeping all of these things alive.

Easter in France is a time to prepare wonderful meals for loved ones – in Britain of course it becomes a contest of who can fit the most chocolate into their mouths. Chocolate which, for some reason, British parents tell their children is delivered by a large rabbit, thus encouraging them to take food from animals.

Summer

Typified by cool, changeable temperatures, drizzle and occasional sunshine, the summer is when the British leave their country en masse to go somewhere hotter and better. To minimize the chances of having to learn another language, the British have set up various havens around the world, such as the Costa Blanca, Gibraltar and Australia.

With the lowest holiday entitlement in Europe, the British holiday appears to be one of the most stressful attempts at relaxation I have ever witnessed, as children are dragged through airports, couples argue and families attempt to fit in as much 'holiday' as possible in the short time allowed. However, to minimize this stress, many Britons will book themselves an 'all-inclusive' holiday package, where everything is included for one cost and they are told what to do, where to be and at what time. This is so that they can consolidate all their complaints and send it to one address at the end of it all, before returning home for a skin cancer assessment.

The British, unlike the French, are unable to enjoy normal daily life, seeing the average weekday as something that must be tolerated or 'got through' while missing any opportunities for pleasure. The weekend or the summer holiday is, to them, the only window of opportunity for enjoyment and so much pressure has been applied to this concept that, by the time such things arrive, they are naturally a disappointment.

At the end of summer, Britain usually feels the need to begin advertising Christmas in shops.

Autumn

Typified by cool, changeable temperatures, drizzle and occasional sunshine, this is when the British have finished attempting to convince themselves and others of how they truly made the most of their summer break. By now it is time to start getting concerned instead about the festive period, still months away. As if this is not enough of an excuse for children to justify unreasonable demands, autumn brings them two more opportunities, in the form of Hallowe'en and 'Guy Fawkes Night'. With or without a costume, a British child denied confectionery can be a terrifying sight and one never knows if it is carrying a knife. Around this time it is best to carry some sweets at all times, to be safe.

Autumn is the time when one can observe several British men performing a task that embodies daily British life as a whole – the ritual sweeping away of leaves into neat piles, soon to be disturbed by the weather or children, before the process begins all over again.

Winter

Typified by cool, changeable temperatures, drizzle and occasional sunshine, winter is a time for the British to complain about a large number of things – the weather (which has become marginally colder than usual), the stress of Christmas and other people in general, as the light literally ebbs out of their lives.

The British go crazy for Christmas, pursuing once again the notion of American capitalism to its full extent. In France, we prefer to celebrate the New Year, as a time of reflection and contemplation over what has passed and what is to come, rather than what a fictional obese man will put in our socks. I have always felt that the passing of time is a far greater cause for celebration than any religion – religion has been the cause of death for so many people over the years. Although, I suppose time is just as guilty of this. If not more so.

Valentine's Day, as capitalist as Christmas in Britain, gives men the opportunity to notice women, compliment them and give them gifts, suggesting they have failed to do so for the past 364 days. Cards contain an array of pre-written sentiments, so that the British do not have to write any romantic verse of their own.

There was an old tradition in France, the *'loterie d'amour'*, which is sadly no more. Men and women would visit the house opposite their own, pairing up with someone from that house. Any man who did not approve of his pairing could leave to find another woman, and any women remaining single would throw images of hurtful past lovers onto a large bonfire, while shouting curses. Women, as usual, took things a step too far and the ritual was banned by the government. A real shame. Although I suppose this would cost me a fortune in photographic reprints for various demanding women.

TOP 10
Phrases You Are Likely to Hear From British Holidaymakers

1. 'How many raincoats should I pack?'

2. 'Do you think they'll have chips there?'

3. 'Darling, we're not allowed to call them that any more.'

4. 'Six bieros por vous plaît.'

5. 'SIX BIEROS POR VOUS PLAÎT.'

6. 'Stop poking it dear, that won't make it pedal us any faster.'

7. 'No, here it's rude if you DO tip. Best not.'

8. 'Well I'm sure it'll go brown afterwards, as long as it doesn't all peel off.'

9. 'I don't think Ouzo is technically a contraceptive.'

10. 'Of course it'll work out. Alonso will love Birmingham. He told me he'd start saving for a flight next week. I miss him already. They're bound to need more fishermen in West Bromwich, right?'

TOP 10
Forgotten Pub Names

1. The Dog and Racist

2. The Queen's Breasts

3. The King's Breasts

4. Ye Olde Slapper

5. The Frosty Welcome

6. The Coffin Dodger's Retreat

7. Paddy O'Stereotypes

8. The Startlingly Mediocre Menu

9. The Pint of Warm Piss

10. The What The Fuck Are You Looking At

Eye Spy Game

Dans La Rue

Rules of the game: points are awarded for rarer sights. See how high you can score.

'But surely it differs according to which town I am in?' you ask. No, no. 96 percent of British high streets are virtually identical.

For this game you will need: eyes.

SHOUTING MAN

The British are a shouty nation. Ironic, considering they have so little to shout about. In fact, actual words will often be omitted completely, replaced instead with animalistic noises.

tick as you spot …

☐	'Oi oi!'	5 points
☐	Other non-specific vowel sounds	5 points
☐	Drive-by shouting	10 points
☐	Shouting/whistling at a top-heavy woman	10 points
☐	Loud talking into an earpiece	15 points
☐	Loud talking into an earpiece just as phone rings, revealing earpiece to be fake (this is a joy to witness)	50 points
☐	'Run, Forrest, run!' (at a running man)	20 points
☐	'Run, Forrest, run!' (at no running man, do not get too close)	50 points

ORANGE WOMAN

Do not be afraid, this woman is not radioactive. In fact, she probably believes Sellafield to be a supermarket. She is part of a curious breed of females who believe that painting themselves a certain shade of orange will result in them resembling movie stars. They are correct, in a way, although 'Garfield' perhaps was not their intended look. Alas, these women are becoming more common in Britain, it seems, so the score is low, although different shades will score you different points.*

☐	Nectarine	5 points
☐	Tangerine	10 points
☐	Finest brandy	15 points
☐	Rabbit sick	20 points
☐	Brass goblin	25 points

* Extra points: 5 for a short skirt, revealing orange skin with realistic orange peel texture. 10 for the very rare long skirt variety.

METROSEXUAL MAN

It is no wonder the British have no masculine and feminine tense – the lines are often blurred. The metrosexual man dresses like a gay but is not one, and still expects to procure women. Truly bizarre.

A full metrosexual will gain you 15 points, but you must observe all the features:

☐	Hairstyle like a startled rodent	5 points
☐	Small bag over the shoulder (with enough space for hair products, walkman and a shit hat)	5 points
☐	Jeans tighter than physics will allow†	5 points

† Bizarrely, despite being unbearably tight, these jeans may also be loose enough at the waist to hang down to the lower buttocks. 5 extra points to spot a pair of dangerously garish underpants beneath the jeans.

Eye Spy Game - Dans La Rue

SHOP PUN

The British do not trust a fish shop or a barber shop unless it has a pun or a 'play-on-words' in its title. For them, it is a mark of quality if they are forced into a weak smile while stepping through the door of such an establishment.

Yet surely these are the shops that require the least humour to guarantee custom. If you must name shops with joke names, why not the funeral parlour (e.g. GRAVE NEW WORLD), the sexual disease clinic (THE PLACE TO BE SPOTTED) or the sperm donation shop (COME FUCK YOURSELF)?

Here are some you are more likely to find:

HAIR SHOPS

A Cut Above The Rest	10 points
Curl Up And Dye	15 points
Cut It You Slag	20 points

FISH SHOPS

The Best Plaice	10 points
The Codfather	15 points
Battered Senseless	20 points
For Cod's Sake; Will Salmon Just Plaice Their Love Mussel In My Battered Clam	25 points

POUND SHOPS

No British high street is complete without at least 6 shops selling every item within for only £1. Most items are of no use at all to the average human.

☐ £1 shop   5 points

☐ 99p shop (the British cannot resist a bargain)   10 points

☐ £1 shop with 2-for-1 offer (depressing)   15 points

CHARITY MUGGER

You WILL be approached by one of these creatures, so it is almost pointless to include this in the game, as they will surely launch themselves at you immediately, like a ninja magpie. Often they are persons in the advanced stages of verbal dysentery, knowing each 'sale' will get them a commission.

Occasionally, the charities are wily and will place an attractive female on the street. In this instance it is worth signing up in exchange for a telephone number. They will always sleep with you that same night when asked, as they know how rejection feels.

The charities are usually for 'cute' children or animals, as the public is more likely to give to these, so more points are awarded for less sellable charities.

☐ Cats/dogs/horses   5 points

☐ Children   5 points

☐ Vagrants   15 points

☐ AIDS   40 points

TOP 10
Bizarre British Laws

It was Jacques Rousseau who said, 'Man is born free, yet everywhere he is in chains.' Judging by some of the ridiculous laws that are still in existence in Britain, it is probably legal to place a man in chains, as long as it is on the first Thursday of a 30-day month, he is a haberdasher and you need to piss.

1. It is illegal to hail a taxi in London if you have the plague

Symptoms of the plague included a stumbling motion, spots on the face and a swelling in the groin. Taxi drivers must face a regular dilemma every Friday and Saturday night when picking up the young men of Britain. 'Bubonic' is yet to pass into the English language to describe a good night out, but give it time ...

2. It is illegal to die in the Houses of Parliament

I am sure this is simply discouraged rather than 'illegal', being a little difficult to enforce, surely. Apparently, being a royal building and therefore better than other buildings, anyone dying within its walls is entitled to a state funeral. This would, of course, prove embarrassing if it was revealed that public money was being spent on the celebration of an old politician who simply sat there for decades passing more bowel gas than policies.

3. It is legal to murder a Scottish man within the city walls of York if he is carrying a bow and arrow

I do not know much about law, but surely the family of the dead Scottish man would have to hire the world's most terrible lawyer for the man of York to get away with this. The clue is in the word 'murder'. And people wonder why there is such animosity between the countries. Not only do Scottish people have to put up with the constant hilarity of the English trying to 'do' their accent, it seems they can also be murdered. Although, frankly, one should be wary of any man carrying a bow and arrow in a town centre.

4. The Welsh are banned from the city of Chester after sunset and before sunrise

While it is very unlike the English to bear a grudge, nobody has thought to overturn this 1403 law, back when the English were rightly terrified of the Welsh, whose land they had attempted to steal for centuries. Nowadays, one would think the Welsh had better things to do than to ransack the city of Chester after sunset. Although, I have seen Swansea in the evenings and I am not sure this is necessarily the case.

5. If a dead whale is found on the British coastline, the head is property of the King and the tail the property of the Queen

Not content with ruling over swans, the monarchy, it seems, can also claim a larger floating creature as their own. I am a little suspicious of there being some typically English play-on-words happening here – the Prince is entitled to have Wales, as long as the King and Queen are allowed whales.

6. It is illegal to fly a kite in the city of London

Useful to know when attempting to relax in a park surrounded by the irritating pestilence of children. Simply wait and then make a citizens' arrest. Britons of the Victorian era believed kites spread disease, which explains this law. However, most of them probably felt the same about homosexuals and black people. This belief is still continued to this day in many parts of South West England.

7. A pregnant woman is entitled to urinate in a policeman's helmet

Finally, the design of the British policeman's helmet explained. Well, it was certainly not designed this way for aerodynamic factors. I wonder, though, if the policeman turns out to be in fact a pervert in disguise, can both be arrested? Him for impersonating a police officer, her for urinating in a non-designated place?

8. It is against the law to book into a London hotel under a false name for the purpose of sex

This is one law of which I have made a special note. Usually the name I use is my own, but from now on I shall be taking on a pseudonym every time to add an element of peril to the encounter.

9. A man is allowed to urinate in public if he keeps his right hand on the vehicle and pisses on the right wheel

Another law involving piss and the police, this time a little less directly. I hope this law clarifies that it must be one's own car involved. And why the *right* wheel? Is the left reserved for women with a good aim? Judging by an average night in London, many cars seem to be in disguise these days as telephone boxes, lifts and public monuments. However, it is unlikely that 'I am sorry officer, I thought it was a car' will suffice when caught using this stance to piss against a police station, or officer.

10. A postage stamp placed upside down is an act of treason

A truly pathetic attempt by the monarchy to claw back some potency. Of course, the average royal is so unintelligent one can surely just explain to them that it is the letter that is upside down, not the stamp. Like the monarchy's family tree, it is all relative.

Animals of Britain

Children of Britain are taught from an early age that their beloved British animals are cute and loveable little creatures, scampering around and doing good, but of course they are in fact waiting to bite your legs, or at least scatter faecal landmines in your path.

The red squirrel

It is said that this squirrel has been supplanted by the American grey squirrel. Yet another example of Britain's insular fear of anything beyond its shores. While every nation should of course distrust anything exported from America, this is a myth. The red squirrel has simply turned himself grey to blend in with the rest of England's mediocrity. As if to eat only nuts is not mediocre enough, this buck-toothed idiot has also slipped on a grey cardigan. We can blame America for many things, but not this.

A mediocre animal

The badger

These dirty little monochrome bastards spend most of their time hanging around the bins, like sex criminals. And yet, for some bizarre reason, they are revered and protected in England, even though they would bite off your foot, given the chance. In France, we beat them at their own game and cook them. Know your place, badgers.

The puffin

Lazy idiot

Puffins can fly, but generally choose not to. We do not accept aquaphobic fish or barkless dogs, so why birds that do not fly? Also, they are friendly to humans for no reason. Puffins, you fat bastards, if you tasted better and were not 'endangered' we would eat you. That child approaching you with a mobile phone does not wish to photograph you – he plans to 'happy slap' you and film it, for being stuck-up and living on your own island. Fucking puffins.

The Manx cat

What a dick. I am not surprised this cat is so pissed off. It has no tail and lives on the Isle of Man, where most human inhabitants appear so unevolved they should own a tail themselves. They are said to be cute (the cats, not the people), despite displaying their arseholes to the world. If a human were to do this, they would be imprisoned, sectioned or selected for the television show *Big Brother*. I will leave you to consider which fate is worse. Manx cat, get out of my sight. But wait until I have turned around, so I don't have to see your anus.

The bee

If an overweight woman told you to embark on daily treacherous missions to procure food for her and protect her with a small knife that would also rip you in half if you ever used it, would you oblige, or would you take advantage of your wings and fly yourself free from the bonds of servitude? If you opt for the latter, congratulations, you are normal. If you choose the first option, you are a bee. Assert your masculinity and realize that, not only are you spending your life chasing after a woman, she is clearly seeing thousands of other bees behind your thorax. She is thousand-timing you. Plus, that honey you're spending every waking hour to produce – do you think it's going to the colony? Bullshit. It will end up on some prick's toast or all over the face of a small child. Wake up and smell the pollen. If you haven't killed yourself trying to collect it ...

The fox

Shut up, shut up, shut up. I know you are fucking. We all know you are fucking. I have had more sexual partners than you, fox, but I do not tell my entire neighbourhood. At most, I will share the graphic details of the night before with a close friend, perhaps with a Polaroid picture or two, but I will not spend the entire liaison yelling at the top of my voice as though my scrotum is trapped in powerful machinery. In France, our foxes do their sex in the woods, like a normal animal. Why in Britain do they insist on a nocturnal vacation to a built-up area to alert the maximum amount of people of their exploits? If you can only get aroused with others listening, at least sound like you are enjoying it.

Noisy fuckers

The hedgehog

Encouraging knife crime all over Britain, these overly defensive creatures carry 5,000 little daggers around with them every day. Get over yourselves hedgehogs, you do not need so much protection. And apparently I cannot let off fireworks or set alight a bonfire on Bastille Day without checking that you are not hibernating. If you wish to sleep for this long, either go underground or get yourselves a job as a postman in Britain. At least then you can double up as a letter opener. Finally an actual use for your spikes.

Animals of Britain

TOP 10

Things in Britain That Look Like Boobs

As a red-blooded human male I am happy to admit that one of the most pleasing sights in life is that of a well-formed titty. In Britain, not only do they name a common breed of bird after nature's life-givers, they pay unsubtle tribute to them in many walks of life.

1. Shuttlecocks

An unlikely shape to be used in any sport, one might think, until one hears that the game of badminton was invented by British military officers while stationed in India, clearly finding innovative ways to deal with missing their wives. Putting the word 'cock' in the title must have been a way of avoiding any defamation against their masculinity.

2. Mushrooms

I believe there are similar codes of conduct when it comes to mushrooms and boobs: it is best to avoid the spotted ones, bigger does not necessarily mean more enjoyable and grabbing a handful before full maturity has been reached can lead to nasty problems.

3. Iced gems

A curious little miniature biscuit largely aimed at children. Especially children, I assume, who were not so long ago attached to the end of their mother's boob, these biscuits being the same size and shape as the average nipple of a lady below room temperature.

4. Police headwear

How the police expect to have any authority in Britain is a mystery to me, when this is what is placed upon their heads.

5. Ancient monuments on hills

'Ah, two stone monuments on two perfectly-domed man-made hills. This must be a sacred site.' So goes the British way of thinking, failing to postulate that this could have been nothing more than something for Celtic men to snigger about.

6. Tea cosies

Recognizing the nurturing power of boobs, Britons use their form to protect their prized possession, the teapot.

7. Christmas puddings

The British tend to forego the traditional Yule log in favour of a boob-shaped pudding. Often they are so disappointed with their own efforts that they will set it on fire, then accompany it with an overly sweet alcoholic butter to take away the taste.

8. Conkers

The seeds of the horse chestnut tree are vaguely nipple-like in character, but British children show an uncharacteristic disdain for them by smashing them together as part of a playground game. Children who do not remove them from their spiky overcoat tend to grow up to be S & M enthusiasts.

9. The Royal Albert Hall

Named in honour of Prince Albert, it is surprising the designers did not choose a more cylindrical design instead, with a metal bolt through the top of it. Appropriately, it was used as the venue for the 'Miss World' competition for two decades. The government of 1999 attempted to repeat the success of the Albert Hall with the Millennium Dome, but it was far less voluptuous and so the public soon lost interest.

10. 'Moobs'

Usually I find the British tendency to disfigure its own language an irritation, but this compound of 'men' and 'boobs' did raise a smile. It is a sign that Britain's obesity levels are reaching worrying highs, when words are invented to describe the size of a man's breasts.

ASK MARCEL

2

Dear Marcel, For some time now I've been suffering from premature ejaculation. It's not just with lovers, sometimes just a badly-fitting trouser or some turbulence on a flight is enough to set me off. While I am sure this is not something that's ever troubled you, I was wondering whether you had any advice.

– Leo Owen-Conway, Staines

Marcel Says: Well, I am man enough to admit that this has occurred to me once, during a weekend with some bad absinthe and some good marijuana. Fortunate for me was that it was on a Pacific island where word would not spread of this lapse in libido. Anyway, you have asked for my advice and so, like you, I will come to a hasty conclusion. I assume you have attempted the usual methods – thinking of a dead relative, etc. Some say the drug Viagra is an option, but surely in your case it will delay your misery, not your sexual encounter. You will be left with a cannon but no ammunition. You will also find it a hindrance if you sleep face-down. If you own a water bed, certainly avoid this drug. But, like a good partner during foreplay, I think perhaps it is all in the head.

Do as I did in this situation and treat sex like a game – a game you always win. You can say, 'Bang! There you go. My personal best is eight seconds. And getting better all the time ...' With luck she may be confused for long enough for you to make another attempt.

Marcel

Culture and Cuisine

'To accept mild Cheddar is to give up on life.'

Sport

It is a sad truth of human nature that an alarming number of persons are still amused intensely by other people kicking, hitting or headbutting things into, over or around other things. This could be a major factor for any observing intergalactic aliens still not bothering to contact us. However, the British not only succumb to this institutionalized idiocy, they in fact regularly allow it to rule their lives. Sometimes, if one man has failed to kick, hit or headbutt a thing correctly in the allotted time, a British man may inflict a similar physical punishment to the face of another man, even though he himself had no control over this original event and is using this sporting failure upon which to project his own life's failures.

In England, during a major sporting competition, especially football, the minds of the masses are focused on nothing else, and one cannot pass a pub without a large sign reading, for example, 'ENGLAND 2010', to remind the stupid bastards which country and year they are in.

Armchair sportsmen

It is not uncommon for a British man, especially an English man, to take credit for a team's efforts, somehow attempting to pass them off as his own, for example:

'*We* are playing football today ... *We* will win because *we* are wearing the red shirt ... *We* were shit against Algeria ..' Well, yes, *you* were. *You* sat on your sofa, farting and shouting at the television. I cannot see that you helped *your* team in any way. It does not work the other way:

'*We* failed to satisfy my wife tonight ..' Although, given the nature of the England football team, they have probably tried to fuck your wife, the dirty bastards.

Football

When it comes to national triumphs, the English are a lot more proud of the year 1966 than another year ending in '66 ... Football has such a hold over the British that it is seen as a perfectly legitimate excuse for absence from work, behaviour even worse than usual when overseas and sharing a woman between several men (why not simply enjoy this act in itself?).

All cheer if you like individualism

To uphold its reputation as 'the beautiful game', it seems players often attend classes in acting and ballet to create a truly melodramatic dive, even when another player's boot is nowhere near their own.

Unlike the Welsh, it is forbidden for the English to sing chants in tune or harmony, however simple those chants are. Popular English chants include 'Who Are You?' (not as existentialist as it sounds) and 'Who's The Wanker In The Black?' (more rhetorical than it sounds). Players' sexuality may be frequently questioned too, and although racist shoutings can now lead to eviction, many football crowds are thankful that 'ginger' is yet to be qualified as a race.

The most well-known English team is Manchester United, 90 percent of whose 'fans' have never in fact attended a game at their home ground. They named as Player of the Century the French player Eric Cantona, whose skills included the kicking of penalties, free kicks and racists. His flair, spirit and elegance have left the British game severely lacking and fans must contend now with idols whose finest traits include marrying failed singers, being unnaturally tall and sleeping with elderly prostitutes.

The World Cup 2010 was seen as a failure for both France and England, although the way I see it, in France a 'striker' means something quite different, namely one who brings about the end of a debate by decisive actions. Therefore, Anelka achieved the best possible result after all the team's altercations and ended the whole ridiculous affair as quickly as possible. A French man knows better than to let a stupid ball game get in the way of a really good dispute.

Foosball

For a nation so addicted to football, and so focused around the pub, there is a true lack of foosball tables in British establishments, often leading to the British challenging Europeans to games in their own countries, only to face a heavy defeat. Much like the real thing.

Rugby

In the spirit of creating yet more ways for academic failures at school to compete against one another, while still feeling like a valid member of society, albeit a society of grunting idiots, the game of rugby has been given many forms. The most popular, 'Rugby Union', is second in popularity only to football. To many of the Welsh, Rugby Union is the more popular, the grunting involved being perfect for a nation with so many consonants at its disposal. Rugby was essentially started by a member of the upper classes cheating at football. You will perhaps notice an English trend here – instead of being reprimanded for this move, the game was made a national sport.

Golf

Just as pantomime is, for the British, a way of justifying the enormous latent urge for transvestism, so golf is a way to justify dressing oneself like a dick. To maximize the pleasure gained from this, the game is stretched out as long as possible, although 'dickmobiles' are provided for those unwilling to walk too far, simply proving that the 'sport' of this pursuit is second to the attire. They name the sticks 'clubs' to try and gain some masculinity from the practice, but it will take more than this to balance out patterned socks that high, trousers that short and polo shirts that pink.

Cricket

Another sport where the attire is entirely unsuitable. In a game where players are expected to slide, tumble and rub a bright red ball vigorously next to the penile area of a trouser, some idiot decided that the official clothing should be entirely white. I am truly surprised that enough British people have the patience for a game that can last almost a week.

Tennis

Believed to have originated in France (once again, you are welcome ...), tennis is another sport that causes hysteria in the English, solely for a concentrated two week period before everybody once again forgets about it. In Wimbledon, the English have created its most famous venue, so that over the decades spectators have been able to jeer at frustrated Americans, buy overpriced strawberries and watch their own national players lose spectacularly. Every 30 years or so the Queen will pay a visit to Wimbledon, to show to her patriotic subjects that she has not lost her ability to wave.

Badminton

Gay tennis.

Boxing

The human body has evolved over the years to become a remarkable entity of organs working in harmony to create movement, respiration and digestion amongst many others, not to mention the mysterious chambers of the conscious and subconscious mind, all of which combined have led humanity to this very point in the time and space of the universe. So what better way to celebrate this than with two grown men doing their best to beat the other back into a primordial form?

But do not fear, rules of fair play exist, outlining exactly how a man must hit another man fully in the face, written by a man who led to the imprisonment of one of Ireland's finest writers, Oscar Wilde. And after his sentence, where did Wilde flee to escape the philistine inhumanity of his former home of England? To France, of course ...

Darts

In Britain, bizarrely, many sports are linked inextricably with drinking large quantities of beer – in fact in Ireland this will ensure you an airport bearing your name – but nowhere is this more blatant than darts. In Britain, a man with larger breasts than the average woman is allowed to call himself a 'sportsman'. In Japan, such men would be forced to wear nappies and fight, in France such men would be American tourists. But in Britain they throw sharp objects at a wall, win trophies, then die of heart disease.

Wacky

Snooker

Said to have been invented in India by officers of the British Army, it is easy to see the popularity of a game involving a white pushing around lots of other colours until they are backed into a corner. Like darts, it is often centred around drinking, but with a certain moderation in comparison – snooker players have to bend over without being out of breath and a waistcoat can only contain a certain amount of waist. At least this sport has a smarter dress code than most.

This, of course, does not mean there are no 'characters' in the world of snooker – over the years players have had some hilarious affectations, such as wearing spectacles the wrong way up, fixing matches for vast sums of money, and assaulting a 14-year-old boy.

In many pubs of Britain, one can find a pool table – a snooker table would require the removal of fruit machines, quiz machines and drunks to fit it in. It is known as 'pool' because, like Britain's municipal swimming pools, it is rarely worth the money, one must wait for idiots to finish their turn and the experience is often ruined by children.

British Bulldog

A game played by school children, I assume to teach them of Britain's current war policy with America, as it chiefly involves a large number of bigger boys charging at a small unwilling boy to achieve 'victory'.

The French alternative – boules

If you really need to satisfy a competitive urge and wish for something more active/less taxing on the brain than chess, what better than a game of pétanque? One gets to be outdoors without looking like a court jester, alcohol and cigarettes can be enjoyed throughout, and the joyous sound of two boules colliding makes for a more pleasant alternative to the crunch of a man's skull. A round of boules can be played anywhere, with healthy discussion encouraged throughout. Don't be a fool – choose boules.

TOP 10
Ridiculous British Trends

As should be clear by now, the British are prone to following the most baffling self-imposed rules and cultural contradictions. Here I shall list some of the more bizarre trends that one can spot in modern Britain. Many arise, of course, from that 'special relationship' between Britain and the USA. It is worth noting that, in English, the word 'special' carries two meanings, one being positive, the other, as is the case here, not so much. In this case, for 'special', think back to the boy at the back of your class attempting to eat the desk. Britain tries constantly to mimic America, and look at how this is repaid over there – at the time of writing, Americans are saying, 'Oh, it is BRITISH Petroleum causing all the damage. Fuck you, the British, we will not buy from you'. I cannot wait for the French to piss off America and see how long those fat bastards last without our fries.

1. The low trouser

British youths have finally sunk to the level of apes, displaying their backsides to the world, as trousers (and, I assume, the British belt industry) reach ever-lower depths. I am told this trend comes from American gangsters, who are not permitted to wear belts in prison. Yet surely the lower the trouser the more likely a 'surprise prison cuddle' from behind? In my opinion, this should be the penalty for such ridiculous trouser management. That would teach them.

2. The false titty

In summer, when clothing becomes minimal, I find I am often in trouble for looking at women, with my hands. From this, alas, I have discovered that so many British women are *buying* new tits. Where I am from, false titties are something one buys in a joke shop. Truly, I don't trust the plastic titty – I fear if I am rubbing my head in between them on a carpet I will get an electric shock, unless one of us is wearing rubber boots. Fortunately, the last time this occurred, she was. The kinky bitch. One time, on an aeroplane, I asked to move seats as I was next to a woman with false titties the size of *pamplemousses* (see page 133). 'I am offended,' I say to the air hostess, 'you take away from me my bottle of absinthe, but allow *these*! Which is the most likely to cause an explosion on this aeroplane?'

3. The emo

Again, I feel you have America to thank for this shadowy, shuffling creature. 'Emo' is supposed to be a shortened form of the word 'emotional', but every drop of emotion seems to have been drained from them. The causes for their morose nature are perhaps a feeling that society does not understand them, a teenage hormonal imbalance or the realization that they will never be able to remove their tight-fitting black trousers without a surgical procedure.

4. Karaoke

And now it is the turn of the Japanese to deposit an indelible influence on your cultural carpet. 'Karaoke', a Japanese word meaning 'song torture', has been repelling and attracting customers to pubs and bars in equal measure for some time in Britain. What began as a way of proving that alcohol intake is proportional to one's perceived vocal talents, has now become an actual night out for many a British idiot. Equally alcohol-induced spectators will often convince the karaoke-ist to re-enact the same humiliation on national television where, with an expression of absolute shock, they are told by people who have actually witnessed live music outside their local pub, that they are as deluded as they are repugnant.

5. The tattoo

Not a solely British trend, of course, but deployed in a more distinct and vulgar way in Britain, by people who were not given enough crayons to play with as a child. For lower-class Britons, especially males, tattoos are like the bright markings of a dangerous creature, instructing others to keep their distance. For those of the middle class it is a way of marking out their individuality, by having exactly the same thing printed in exactly the same place as everyone else – a spirally ring around the upper arm for men and an oriental symbol above the buttocks for women, which might as well mean 'easy'.

6. The mobile phone idiot

In the 1980s teenagers would carry with them loud stereo systems larger than an average dog, yet somehow these were less irritating than a British youth beeping his way through his 'apps', marvelling at the revolutionary function of taking a photograph and allowing an entire bus to hear what music would sound like if made by hyperactive underwater drummers with no musical training.

7. Dressing like a prick on purpose

This practice is mainly confined to London, although in more remote parts of Britain it is unclear whether the locals are attempting to follow London trends, or simply blissfully unaware of what they are wearing. In a painfully shallow attempt at postmodernity, or postpostmodernity, or whatever, the middle classes (especially those involved in media) have found an innovative way to save money for drugs – by buying terrible clothes from charity shops, cutting their own hair and forming a self-regulating 'gang' where this is deemed a fashion statement rather than the abomination it is.

8. 'Like'

Many times in Britain I am suspicious that I am in fact part of some elaborate prank, none more so than when in the presence of teenage girls. On top of entirely unnatural inflections in sentences, the word 'like' will be thrown in at any given juncture, regardless of any reference to something they 'like' or something that is 'like' something else. It is no wonder Britain records such high teenage pregnancy statistics. If the girls are saying 'like' as often as this, surely this is just giving encouragement to the boys?

9. The language of the text message

Another part of the coded language of the British teenager, but sadly also adopted by those who are older and should know better. Originally a way of abbreviating interjections to save space on text messages, it is now being used in everyday speech, despite saving nothing on syllables. To confuse things further, there are variations. I have been told by two different sources that the ubiquitously irritating 'LOL' can mean 'Lots Of Love' *and* 'Laugh Out Loud' – surely a problem when responding to any text concerning tragic news from a friend? 'LOL from me' in its latter form is simply inappropriate as a response to 'My grandfather has just died.'

10. The inappropriate 'legging' wearer

Women of Britain, it should be my choice whether I get to see your vagina. Too many times I have turned a corner in a British town during summer time, to be presented by the full outline of a (usually obese) woman's lower torso, with every fold and contour outlined perfectly thanks to this woman's refusal to wear a skirt. Not only does the legging sound like some lesbian manoeuvre, it is usually part of some ridiculous combination such as the appropriately-named 'Ugg' boot, a functionless belt or flagrant obesity.

Eye Spy Game

Dans Le Pub

Rules of the game: points are awarded for rarer sights. See how high you can score.

The British pub is a haven for those seeking refuge from a spouse, an intellectual debate or their own mind. I will occasionally choose a pub over a civilized bar or art space if I need to feel better about myself.

For this game you will need: eyes.

FREAKISH BAR SNACKS

A barman will employ any trick to keep his customers thirsty and until beer scientists invent a drink that somehow manages to create this effect itself, snacks of unnatural saltiness can be found behind any British bar.

☐ Peanuts	5 points
☐ Pork scratchings (terrifying)	5 points
☐ Nuts in unpleasantly spicy casing	10 points
☐ Snack unknown to barman resembling a squirrel's ballbag	15 points

PUB GAMES

British people, understandably, often tire of one another's conversation. Games are sometimes provided in pubs to rectify this, whether the space within that pub is suitable or otherwise. Naturally, these are rarely games requiring the use of the brain, such as chess or backgammon, but rather games that fulfil the desire to hit things or press a button to lose more money.

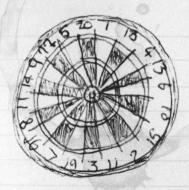

☐ Pool table	5 points
☐ Pool table with all balls present	10 points
☐ Dartboard	5 points
☐ Darts	15 points
☐ Fruit machine	5 points
☐ Man winning more than he has put in	20 points

BEER GARDEN ☐   5 points

Usually a misnomer, of course, unless one counts as a 'garden' some concrete, a few benches and an umbrella, situated next to a car park.

UNNECESSARY OLD BIT ☐   15 points

An older pub will often be so overly keen to describe itself as the Oldest Pub in the County/Country/World/Universe that, although it has clearly been renovated over the centuries it will retain a part of its original structure. Perhaps a beam or rafter, a barrel that has never been changed or the original owner's teeth.

BAR CLEAVAGE 🔲   10 points

Every landlord knows that it is not simply the arid bar snacks or the flashing lights of an electronic pub game that will keep the men of his establishment returning to order drinks – the mysterious trench of a woman's chest is more alluring than all of these things. This is especially true for men who are unused to a woman remaining there for more than five seconds when he engages them in conversation. The fact that she is paid to does not dampen such a man's spirits. In fact, the more drinks she serves to him the more he believes he is in with a chance, in a cruel cycle of testosterone, alcohol and feminine manoeuvres.

RESIDENT DRUNKARD

What we French would call *une éponge* (a sponge), this man has indeed attempted to soak up any liquor within his reach. To make

room for the alcohol, his brain must jettison useless and trivial facts via his mouth to anyone who will listen. In fact often a second person is not even required. He is likely to have a complete knowledge of all local ales, having witnessed every single one come and go for years.

🔲 Belch   5 points

🔲 Belch with 'bits'   10 points
(at this point avoid sitting too close)

🔲 Sexist/homophobic/racist comment   10 points
(5 extra points if said within a belch.)

🔲 Fall from stool   20 points

🔲 Attempt to order another drink as
though nothing has happened   5 points

AMERICAN TOURISTS ☐   10 points

Easy to spot. This couple will sit at a table waiting to be served
for an extraordinary amount of time, describing everything they
see as 'quaint' until a fight begins in the corner, concerning a
spilt beer, which, as in a war, the Americans will get involved with
only when it is a little late. Days later they will be extremely
unwell due to an undercooked pub sausage, yet will still describe
the experience as 'quaint'.

TOILET GRAFFITI

A common British phrase is 'talking out of your arse' and many
toilet-visiting Britons seem to have extended this metaphor,
judging by the amount of writing on the walls of public toilets
all over the nation. The signage for male toilets usually reads
'GENTLEMEN', which must cause many travellers to leave Britain
believing that its code of good conduct includes urinating
everywhere but the toilet, before dropping a full toilet roll into
that piss. Here are some witty pieces of badinage you may find
in the 'Gents'.

☐ 'Look left' [on right wall],
   'Look right' [on left wall]   5 points

☐ Telephone number with suggested sexual
   act promised on calling this number   5 points
   (Add a further 5 points for a sexual act of which you have never heard.)

☐ 'I fucked your mum'   5 points

☐ 'Go home Dad, you're drunk' beneath
   the previous scrawling   15 points

I Fucked your Mum!

↓
Go home Dad – you're drunk !!!

Cuisine

Some say the way to a man's heart is via his stomach. They are wrong, of course, it is in fact via another organ prone to filling with blood and providing the occasional attack.* If we are talking literally, though, this saying is true, and the British seem to have tailored the majority of their cuisine to produce a deadly double-strike on these prime locations. Good food is available in Britain, but one really has to seek it out. It is incredible how much the British can get it wrong, even to the smallest degree. For example, fruit and vegetables are widely available, but the British, ever proud of their technology, seem to have managed to cross-breed them with cardboard. The term we use for the gastronomic horror found regularly in British dining establishments is *la malbouffe*. The British simply call it 'lunch'.

The freezer ... the British kitchen's best friend

In my opinion (i.e. the correct one) a freezer should be used only for storing ice in cubed form, for the purpose of placing in cocktails and/or women. In Britain, however, the freezer dominates the kitchen, serving as a large ghostly reminder of the average Briton's ineptitude in this culinary space. Inside it, like a cannibal's trophy cabinet, one will find all manner of horrors. Most of these terrible artefacts will be unrecognizable, as they will be covered entirely in breadcrumbs. For some reason, the British believe this to be acceptable – to cover such atrocities with food that is usually fed to a duck. Encased within these orange-crumbed shells one will find the mashed-up feet, chins and testes of a number of creatures – chickens, turkeys, cows and probably hideous hybrid beasts bred from all three. I am told one may even find a reservoir of cheese within the centre of these

---

* The penis, in case you were unsure.

Frankensteinian abominations. I would not be surprised also if the opposite were available in the average British supermarket – a block of cheese containing a strip of pork, some beef soup or some sheeps' tits.

The Full English Breakfast

It is no surprise that so many English are looking as 'full' as they are if this is their daily breakfast. The French are content to start their day with a light pastry, the British with a coronary. There are variations of course – for the 'Full Scottish' add more oats and pig's blood, for the 'Full Irish' more bread and potatoes, for the 'Full Welsh', bizarrely, some seaweed. The insatiable desire for this dish has led to cafés ignoring civilized convention and serving 'all day breakfasts'.

A hearty (attacky) breakfast

Mild Cheddar

Who the fuck is eating mild Cheddar? I believe this has never been near a cow in its life. Or if it has, the farmer is in the field every day talking to the cow about the weather, boring it into making the cheese more bland and shit. To accept mild Cheddar is to give up on life. He who eats mild Cheddar is saying, 'Everything in my life must be mild. Give to me a mild meal surrounding this mild Cheddar, some mild company, a mild wife, a mild beer, a mild wine' – or even worse, a *mulled* wine (if you wish your wine to be warm with pieces floating in it, simply piss in it). 'How do you like your

Mild Cheddar ... not worth squeezing a cow for

weather?' one might ask this person. 'Oh, mild, thank you,' comes the inevitable reply. They will buy a dog and cut off its balls to make it more mild, then buy it a coat, in case the weather is not mild enough. *This animal already has a coat you stupid fuck!* They will sit at home, with a mild beer or a mild coffee, after a mild day in a mild job, waiting for a mild-life crisis. A good cheese – a Roquefort, a Camembert – will live on in the mouth and the mind for days.

Crisps

Britain boasts an overwhelming array of ways to ruin a potato, mostly in the form of crisps. Walk into a British store of any size (or sports centre) and you would be mistaken for believing the crisp to be the answer to any dietary need, such is its abundance. And, just as the devil is said to take many forms, so does the crisp – round, square, triangular and spherical. Some are even made to appear like bacon, to falsely hint at having any nutritional value at all. In 2009, a famous crisp-maker* held a competition for the British to design a new flavour of crisp (as if there are not already enough!). The winning entry fought off much competition, (including my own suggestion of 'hand'†), and was revealed to be the cryptic 'Builder's Breakfast' flavour. This did not even last a year on the shelves, simply supporting my speculation that most British builders are too lazy to rise for breakfast.

---

* Whose name is in fact a healthy activity not generally associated with its consumers.
† I imagine the company are still ruing their decision not to include my entry in their challenge. Come on! How many packets would have been sold through curiosity alone?

Soft drinks

To wash down this bewildering selection of crisps, Britain has decided that it requires just as numerous a selection of unhealthy beverages. Do not worry, it is still possible to find an Orangina, but not before wading through a vast ocean of sugar and colourings. Via certain 'energy drinks' containing aspartame, Britain has found a way to justify their inhumane working hours and lack of a mid-afternoon rest. Tiredness surely is a body's way of telling us to rest, not to dangerously increase our heart rate by some unnatural means. Along with the Danish and Norwegians, the French have banned this obscene substance, as we realize that, in the long term, our workers taking a brief rest every day is preferable to them dropping dead.

Toad in the hole/Spotted dick, etc.

To match their unappealing food, the British will often choose a suitably unappealing name. For example, to offer a child 'spotted dick' after dinner is seen as a treat, rather than a reason to report a parent to the authorities or have them protected by the Pope. Butterfly cakes contain no such thing, and I at least expected 'toad in the hole' to be some vulgar British attempt to replicate frogs' legs, but no. It is yet another way of introducing batter to a meat product. 'Bubble and squeak' I have not yet dared to venture towards, but if it is as I suspect, then it is some kind of fizzy mouse drink – after what I have seen so far I would be far from surprised.

'Chocolate'

Usually next to the 'crisps' section of a shop, a staggering array of 'chocolate' is to be found, although I think we will have to disagree with our definitions of this food. In France we regard it as a delicacy, a treat to enjoy, made from rich cocoa butter, but in Britain you pollute your chocolate with vegetable fat, presumably so that bad mothers feeding it to their increasingly spherical children can justify it as part of their 'five-a-day'.

Welsh rarebit

When a country describes a combination of bread, cheese and ham as 'rare', one instantly recognizes that one is in culinary trouble.

Irish stew

Now we are talking. Simple, but at least healthy, without any sign of deep-frying, battering or bizarre animal naming. Some more herbs and a little garlic would not go amiss, but I soon learned while visiting Ireland to simply bring my own. If you are to do this, add it once the food has arrived. Not ideal, but I have learned from my mistake of entering the kitchen and handing them directly to the chef.

The pasty

A traditional dish of Cornwall, now officially so since 2002. In France, we have made a point that one cannot simply put some fizzy alcohol in a bottle and call it 'Champagne', whereas in England the Cornish are similarly overprotective of some mushed-up cow, turnips and potatoes in a small pastry handbag. Originally created for miners so that they could carry their food without dirtying it, the pasty is now the ideal food for any Brit who wishes for that ideal 'being a miner' feeling in their life without having to carry out any hard work.

The balti

A curry dish of which the people of the English Midlands are insanely proud, although there is some debate regarding whether it was invented in Birmingham, or the Pakistan area of Baltistan. I shall just repeat that – Birmingham, or *Balti*stan. The English, of course, insist it is the former, but I believe linguistic evidence suggests otherwise. I have visited a balti house and all I will say is this: the one positive element I took from the entire experience was that I was allowed to bring my own alcohol. And yet, I would challenge anyone to find a suitable wine to accompany such a bizarre and unsubtle flavour. It is how I imagine it might feel to kiss a dog on the mouth. I did not venture any further into this culinary terrain, despite being offered a 'chicken tikka masala', suggested by some to be Britain's national dish. It is heartwarming to see Britain realize its own shortcomings when it comes to matters of the kitchen and so 'borrow' from someone else's.

Excessive tea drinking

Britain consumes a ridiculous 165 million cups of tea a day. This obsessive compulsive disorder is used as an excuse for the self-employed to have an unlimited number of breaks, for the middle and upper classes to use painfully brittle cups (whenever their fellow tea drinker is deemed special enough for this privilege) and for general confusion when it comes to the naming of an evening meal. Tea ranks as highly as pets in the British household, with a teapot often being given its own living quarters and clothing. Its popularity can be explained by its original association with the aristocracy, so via tea every Briton can live up to their bourgeois aspirations, even if stirring it with a scratch card.

Fish and chips

Too obvious to mention? Perhaps, but I will do so anyway. It takes an especially culinarily carefree nation to decide that the best thing to do with a subtle food like fish is to throw it in the deep-fat fryer and then add some liquid nuclear peas to give the impression of a balanced meal. Britain, there is only so much help we French can give you.

Alcohol, Cigarettes and Drugs

Alcohol and drugs have always played an essential part in the existence of the British, to remove some monotony from their daily lives, erase memories of epic failures when trying to communicate with the opposite sex (often while under the influence of alcohol or drugs in the first place) and make each other look better (it is rare that any of these effects will last until morning). I have once again thrown myself into the task of investigating this subject, if anything to take away the taste of the British cuisine from the previous section.

Alcohol

The French have a symbiotic relationship with alcohol, giving it the respect and understanding it deserves, and seeing it as a natural accompaniment to intelligent conversation or existentialist debate. The British, it seems, are all raised believing there to be a limited supply, which may expire at any moment during their lifetime and so make it a vital part of their diet, often above all else. Sayings are dedicated to alcohol, such as 'wine and then beer makes you feel queer.' In my experience wine and then beer makes you feel women's breasts without their permission – quite the opposite.

Wine

I heard that the British have started producing their own wine. However, the man who told me that was fairly drunk himself and I believe it to have been a joke.

MARCEL'S WINE TIP ...

If at a British party you find yourself stating a point too exuberantly and, in doing so, spill red wine on a carpet, it is deemed acceptable to then spill white wine on top of it as a cleaning agent, such is the ubiquity of terrible white wine at such functions. And it is no myth - liberally spill the white on the red and it will disappear like magic. It does not, however, work the other way around. This will enrage your host, if anything.

Beer

What the British certainly do specialize in is beer with any sparkle removed, which is then warmed to room temperature. This seems to be especially popular with bearded men, although it is unclear whether or not the drink itself has led to the beard growth.

The Irish go a step further and seem to infuse their beer with tar. They are so desperate to get rid of this beverage that they are constantly trying to sneak it into their cuisine.

The Scottish, however, are the undisputed kings of alcoholism, producing an overwhelming variation of strong spirits, and adding 'super' to the title of their strongest lager, to convince vagrants it will give them special powers.

Whatever they are swilling from bottles in Newcastle and other northern English towns, this does indeed seem to have bestowed certain superpowers upon the residents. Resistant to cold, even in the height of winter, the men survive without coats, and the women largely without dignity, in a constant contest for who can cover the lowest percentage of their bodies. Some appear to have cheated by wearing a kind of orange weather-resistant paint all over (see page 71).

Alcopops

To prepare for the gargantuan drinking contest that their lives will
become, British teenagers begin training early, lured into it by lurid
alcobominations, available in such colours as toothpaste blue, murky
white and mucus green, which at least add a dash of colour to their
lacklustre British dinner once they reach the stomach.

Cigarettes

Remarkably, in a place as unhealthy as Britain, where breakfast cereals are
made of chocolate and even apples can find themselves covered in toffee
and sold to children, the cigarette ban is firmly in place. Even smoking
beneath a tree can lead to tutting.

As someone raised at a time in France when smoking was practically
compulsory, I still find this a difficult law to uphold. Still, I would rather
deny myself a cigarette than be forced into one of the colonies huddled
outside in one of the 'designated areas'. The tutting I can handle, but to
not look cool while smoking renders the practice almost useless.

Drugs

Drugs are, of course, a very useful addition to an artiste's toolbox, and
should only be used by those who will produce something creative as
an end result. Good opium or marijuana (or proper absinthe, seemingly
unavailable anywhere in Britain) have all been the catalyst for many
an epic *oeuvre*. However, in Britain, drugs are often used for quite the
opposite purpose, to avoid the horrifying prospect of saying anything at
all worthwhile.

Cocaine

Cocaine is used mainly by those in the business of media – we know this
because it is the first thing they will tell you when on the drug. In fact,
you will soon learn many things about this person, none of which you ever
wished to. There is a reason for the cutting of cocaine on a mirror – this

chopping board will then be put to its traditional use very soon afterwards, as the cocaine user practices their incessant talking while staring into their own vacuous black-hole eyes.

Ecstasy

So repressed are the English that often they must take a small tablet to enable them to dance, touch their fellow man or smile. Often this results in all three of these things being taken a step too far. One can now buy an ecstasy pill for the price of a sandwich, but unlike the sandwich*, the ecstasy will keep you dancing to repetitive music for several hours, convincing your body that this is a productive use of time, and keep you awake for just as long.

We French are able to maintain a fascinating debate for this long, fuelled simply by wine and intellect, and have increased our knowledge by the following day, rather than losing a large amount of it in the process. We can expend our energy in the bedroom, sharing sweat between two or three people, rather than 500.

Ketamine

Would you pay money to be bewildered by horse drugs? If the answer is 'yes' there is a good chance you are British. For the same price as the Ketamine I will happily take you instead to a stable and discuss the nature of complex existentialism, while idiots dance awkwardly around you and a man beats two barrels very fast with a stick.

Others

I have neither the time nor the inclination to keep up with Britain's ever-widespread drug culture and the phraseology of each new narcotic. My suggestion would be this: if its name is longer than four syllables or sounds like a cartoon character, it is probably best left alone.

* Unless it is a really good sandwich.

Hair of Britain

Men

Facial hair around the world serves many a purpose – to define a face, to attract a mate and, in extreme cases, to store food for the winter. The facial hair of British men sees many trends come and go. A recent resurgence in beard growth gave British men the perfect excuse for laziness. 'Oh, the beard is making a comeback,' many would say. But of course they are idiots – the beard 'makes a comeback' every 5 or 6 days, this is how hair works. Here are some common British styles:

THE REVERSE QUEEN'S GUARD

This man has something to hide. A guilty secret perhaps, a psychopath's smile, or the majority of yesterday's lunch. Either way, he is best avoided for a number of health and safety reasons.

McBEARD

This man is almost definitely Scottish, or attempting to conceal something extremely badly. It is admirable when a Scottish man, not only born with a hair colour that leads to daily near-racial abuse, but bountiful amounts of it, decides to embrace nature and banish any cutting implements from his life. This beard type is usually accompanied by eyebrows that would easily house two nests of starlings and a daily intake of the strongest whisky, which I assume adds a certain sheen to this particular type of beard.

THE STEERING WHEEL

Usually acceptable on any other European man, on a British man something is not quite right here. I don't know why something so chic on the continent should come across as 'untrustworthy' in Britain, but these men are best avoided on this island. Again, for reasons unknown, this man is three times more likely to wear a mobile phone earpiece.

THE FLATTENED HEDGEROW

Another hair type that, for whatever reason, appears untrustworthy. It is highly likely that this man is a teacher of some kind. While unfathomably popular among young British men early in the previous century, since then a certain German man has been responsible for a rapid decrease in the popularity of any upper-lip hair.

THE FULL ENGLISH

This man, if you can make any sense of his ramblings, probably harbours some 'interesting' views regarding people of a different skin colour, homosexuals and women. Fortunately for him his words are largely swallowed up by the dense hair covering the vast majority of his face, hair which also acts as padding should anyone more liberal understand his words and attempt to administer a punch to the face beneath it.

THE LIGHT COATING

An excellent choice. This man is making a bold statement to the world that he has more important things to do in life than hack away small hairs from his face every single morning, while still maintaining a modicum of facial discipline. A woman can appreciate the rough textures brushing her face/neck/thighs, without feeling she is being spring-cleaned by a feather-duster.

Women

As Simone de Beauvoir said, 'A woman was not born a woman, she becomes one.' And indeed, British women, like any others, will go to great lengths to try to achieve this, the hair often being the front line for this battle against nature. But, rather than focus on the hair on a woman's head, which takes on a nauseating amount of permutations, I shall instead focus on the hair which, indeed, is more focused on by man in general – the 'hair down there'. Do not fear, plenty of research has been done for this section of the book. However, to avoid the placing of this book in the wrong section of the bookshop (medical or pornographic), alas I am not permitted to use the original illustrations, and so must instead, with some artistic licence, transplant these lower hairstyles pictorially onto the chins of men once again. Use your imagination.

THE TEASING STRIP

Commonly known as the 'Brazilian', I have found this to be a misnomer, judging by the Brazilian girls I have slept with. It is in fact the American women who will tend to choose this style. They refer to it often as the 'landing strip', which further backs my theory that it is an American design – the American man, he requires guidance to land his plane. Even with a landing strip, he will probably still miss. He may refer to this manoeuvre as 'friendly fire', but without permission to land it won't be so friendly in the morning. This design appears to be the choice of many young British women too, as once again Britain tries to appear fashionable to its big brother America.

THE VANISHING ACT

An increasingly popular choice amongst younger women of Britain, and herein lies the danger. Given the amount of cosmetics worn by teenage girls in this country, how is one to tell if she is legal or not, when faced with this situation?

If she has driven you back to her place, this is a fairly good indication of legality, and you can proceed without fear of recrimination (unless, of course, it is her boyfriend's car). But I am always uneasy when faced with this hairless dilemma. This style, I am told, is known as the 'Hollywood'. This, I assume, is due to the revealing of a vacuous hole once everything is removed from the surface. Of course, it could also be that, when in Hollywood, one is only ever a small distance away from a twat or an arsehole.

JE T'AIME
The classic Valentine's manoeuvre. Usually reserved for a loved one, otherwise it just comes across as desperate. A lover of mine once opted for an Arc de Triomphe shape, providing a wonderful welcome to her Champs Elysées. But, alas, true to life, it had been visited by far too many a tourist.

THE WOOLLY WINTER WARMER
This woman is almost definitely Scottish, or attempting to conceal something extremely badly.

THE TRIANGLE OF LOVE
Ideal. Some hair should certainly be there. Not too much – it should not appear as though it comes with its own washing label – but enough at least to assure you she is legal, and not American. This British obsession for hairlessness in this area is a little troubling. One does not complain about picking the occasional bone from good salmon, so why fear picking the occasional hair from between the teeth? And fans of the British play-on-words may like to approach the triangle by 'trying it at any angle.'

Reality TV

The British are a barbaric and bloodthirsty nation (see snowman treatment, page 133), and since they are now denied the pleasure of imprisoning and torturing princes in towers, they must live this through their television shows. Gone are the days of aspiring to the glamour and panache of the TV and film studios, these days most Britons simply like to feel better about themselves by watching the socially and mentally subnormal performing spurious tasks, being humiliated and occasionally falling in some water. With this in mind, here are some of my pitches for future 'Reality TV' shows on UK TV:

How shit is your life?

Friends must nominate the strongest-willed person they know from their friendship group, who is then visited by a team of experts who criticize everything in their life, eventually breaking them down and forcing them to conclude that everything in their life is shit. Whoever lasts the longest in the series wins a 10-year therapy voucher and a deluxe foot spa.

Trivia wars

The entire population of England, Scotland, Ireland and Wales answer pointless trivia questions to redraw the boundaries of each country. Every household will be issued with a multiple-choice buzzer and each series will last 50 weeks.

How to look better naked

Female viewers have to send me pictures of themselves unclothed, which are then digitally placed on a picture of me unclothed. This, in fact, does not even need to be a TV show, you are welcome to simply send me the pictures anyway. If it does become a show, however, the winner will get to re-enact this scene in real life. There will be at least five winners per show.

Drag queen's den

Eager yet misguided entrepreneurs will announce their business proposals to a table of bitchy and sarcastic drag queens, who will almost entirely ignore their ideas, and instead comment in a snide way about their shoe/jacket combination, hairstyles and general demeanour. There will be absolutely no intention to commission any of their ideas.

Veal, or no meal

Vegan contestants are transported to remote, desolate areas of the world – Antarctica, the Arizona desert, Hull etc. and starved for a day. They are then presented with an array of boxes, which they can choose to open. It soon becomes obvious that every single one contains veal, with the occasional lettuce leaf or onion on the side. A banker will call and offer more veal, with another almost insignificant vegetarian side dish. Contestants will have to question their principles and decide 'veal, or no meal'.

There may be possible moral objections to this one – look into ways of getting around this.

Zidane, you're rocking the boat

Seven contestants are put on a boat, which they are told to row across the channel. Also on the boat is Zinedine Zidane, who will occasionally and without warning rock the vessel from side to side, to try and displace a crew member (the crew will be dressed in cumbersome penguin costumes). Contestants are allowed one attempt each to politely ask Zidane to stop. If a further attempt is made by a rower, the ex-French captain will be allowed instead to headbutt that person into the water. We expect Zidane to become more enraged with every series.

The British Joke

The English have a wonderful age-old tradition of repeating the same joke again and again and again in a distinctly limited number of ways. The humour of the French is too sophisticated to simplify in one or two lines and we have better ways to entertain ourselves than simply exchanging the beginning letter of one word with that of another. Using the templates for every British joke available, I have put my own spin on these tired formulae.

Englishman, Irishman, Scotsman

An Englishman, an Irishman and a Scotsman enter a pub. Due to centuries of deep-seated mistrust they each retire to different corners of the pub, occasionally glancing at one another. When served by an Eastern European at the bar, each man once again retires to his corner, reading *The Daily Mail* newspaper and muttering about foreigners 'taking their jobs', despite all three having been fired from their own jobs due to alcoholism and/or negligence.

Medical joke

Doctor, doctor, I feel like a pair of curtains.

Well I'm afraid there's a 6-month waiting list for this treatment on the NHS. Perhaps in France you would have had a more rapid and effective response, due to the excellent state healthcare provided for its citizens, but as it is, for now you will simply have to pull yourself together.

The London 'knock-knock' joke

Knock knock?

Who is there?

A neighbour.

A neighbour who?

Matthew. I live down the corridor. I just –

Have you got a knife?

Sorry?

Have you got a knife?

No, I was just wondering if I could –

Have we met?

Well, no. I'm in flat 35. We –

You could be anyone.

Do you know Sarah in flat 21?

No.

Michael, flat 17?

No.

Sophie, flat 31?

No.

But that's next door to you.

I don't know them.

I just wanted to borrow a –

You could be a murderer.

I'm not.

What are you?

Actually, I'm a doctor.

Doctor who?

Oh forget it.

What is black and white and red all over?

A British steak, hideously overcooked and ruined further by the addition of mayonnaise and tomato sauce.

What is the difference between an Englishman and a Scotsman?

The Scotsman, he batters the Mars bar; the Englishman, he batters the indigenous population of a country, under the banner 'colonialism', and then berates the Scotsman for battering the Mars bar.

The British Joke   117

Why did the chicken cross the road?

Being a French chicken, it was able to roam freely, on a family-run all-natural farm, ending its days presented beautifully on a plate, served with a rich sauce to compliment its wholesome flavour, unlike its British counterpart, who rarely sees sunlight, let alone a road, living beak-to-beak with several thousand of its unfortunate brethren, who will all end up mushed together, deep-fried, drowned in ketchup and guzzled by an obese and spotty child so unfit that it can barely manage to cross the road to get to the other side.'

Holiday joke

'Waiter, there's a fly in my soup.'

'Sir, this is the least of your concerns, given the distinct lack of herbs, consistency and flavour to this English soup. If anything, it is the one element giving it any real body at all.'

What do you call a man with a spade in his head?

The unfortunate victim of a man who, according to neighbours, 'always seemed such a quiet and lovely man.'

What do you get if you cross a member of the House of Lords' palm with silver?

A life peerage, entitling you to various benefits, and a title suggesting you are better than everyone else, despite being under no obligation to do anything of use for your country.

What do you call a fish with no eyes?

A victim of the battery conditions used in UK fish farms, not to mention the industrial pollution.

How many Englishmen does it take to invent a light bulb?

One, in 1800, only to have an American, of all people, trample over your legacy.

'I say , I say, I say ...

... oh, I appear to have completely forgotten what it was I was going to say, due to my unnecessarily large weekly intake of strong lager.'

What goes 'ha ha bonk?'

A woman mocking her British 'lover's' attempt at lovemaking, before discovering that the French man in the adjacent room, true to his word, can indeed do a much better job, and so pays him several visits throughout the honeymoon.

This one is based on an actual happening, as all the finest jokes are. 'Funny because it's true', as the British would say.

British Pets

In French the word 'pet' means a fart, which I believe to be the only service the average domestic animal brings to the world. OK, I admit, sometimes they will go a stage further and shit. Yet, for some reason, the British actively allow these creatures into their homes. From the 'speed bumps of the pavement' left behind by overly large dogs, to the deceptively trufflesque cat parcels left in gardens and the eery trails that pursue fish after a meal, the British happily accept this as part of their 'special bond' to beasts which any self-respecting homo sapiens should in fact eat.

The dog

The relationship between Britons and their dogs is quite worrying. Within weeks of coming to Britain I had seen an owner allowing his little hairy pride and joy to lick him on the mouth, just minutes after the dog had been licking its own little hairy pride and joy.

Probably carrying: Fleas, mange, an erection to rub up against you.

My 'best friend' has never fucked my leg

The cat

A sneaky beast, that has managed to persuade humans to be its friend over thousands of years. Given a chance, it will instantly revert back to its ancestral status of Lord of the Jungle and eat you. Trust me, if you were to die and remain in your home for longer than an hour with a cat inside, what is in its food bowl would not be its first dining option ...

Probably carrying: Fleas, a dead mouse, cat AIDS.

The rabbit

Hyperactive, high maintenance and capable of chewing through almost anything, I cannot see why anyone bothers having a rabbit as a pet. If it lasts beyond a week, without biting a power cable, drowning in its own filth or having a heart attack, it will only survive longer through a picky diet and having its hair constantly brushed, like a spoilt child. They are also exceptionally good at making new rabbits, so any peace in your house will be interrupted constantly by rabbit-sex.

Probably carrying: Myxomatosis.

Pass me the garlic and herbs

The goldfish

By calling this fish 'gold' the British are attempting to add some false status to a pet so readily available that it is given away at fairgrounds. Usually kept in a bowl just large enough to fit a cat's head, which will contain not only the fish but for some reason a castle, it is difficult to see what the purpose of this creature is as a pet. Do the British public enjoy being the ones who have control over something with a castle for a change? Or perhaps it is the novelty of seeing a fish that has not yet been deep-fried.

Probably carrying: Amoebic gill disease.

The hamster

Ah, the perfect pet for any child – if they pick it up it will either shit on their hand or die of heart failure, if released they will run and hide somewhere completely unreachable and if the child is lucky they can watch one eat its own young. The hamster doesn't even know how to eat, storing as much food as possible in the sides of its mouth, rather than just leaving it for later. If it doesn't trust you enough not to steal its food, then it does not deserve to be living under your roof.

Probably carrying: Plague.

Eye Spy Game

Dans Le Club

Rules of the game: points are awarded for rarer sights. See how high you can score.

For the hardened Eye Spy player, or the terminally bored.

For this game you will need: eyes and a distinct lack of self-respect.

Most British men will tell you that the place to procure women is supposed to be the nightclub. Especially if you are looking for a woman covered in 500 other mens' sweat, who enjoys being shouted at, while deafened by shit music. You will soon grow bored of this stablishment as you observe men attempting to impress women by drinking more than they are technically able, and then forcing their hands up the closest skirt, before being ejected. So here is another visual challenge for you to complete during your time in this loud obnoxious fuckpit.*

---

* Remaining in this place for too long can irreversibly taint your opinion of the worth of the entire human race. Although a healthy misanthropic streak is to be admired in a man, this experience may prove too much, especially as you have now become an accessory to this by paying money to enter. You will also notice that the women who frequent UK nightclubs are very similar to the toilets of the UK nightclubs – they are either engaged or vacant. Some are disabled, but I would feel guilty about using them.

CRYING WOMAN ❏   10 points

In every nightclub is a crying woman. Perhaps a man has
rejected her advances, perhaps she has spotted a woman wearing
identical shoes to her, perhaps she has just drunk enough wine
to realize that she, like every woman, is in fact mentally
unstable. Life is a series of disappointments and then we die.
Get over it, like the rest of us.

LEERING MAN ❏   15 points

There is an exact art to leering, and this man could not be going
about it more badly. Focused intently on the breasts of every
woman in the club, his drool is proportional to the size of breast
he is eyeballing. Alcohol has instructed his brain that this
technique is irresistible to women, while every female reaction
tells him otherwise. There is a large possibility he still lives with
his mother.

(Add an extra 5 points if you spot his inevitable move towards CRYING
WOMAN. Add an extra 5–25 points depending on the violence of her response
to this.)

Eye Spy Game – Dans Le Club

BOUNCER ☐ 5 points

A wonderful name for this guardian of the door, as their size and strength allows them to bounce any undesirables out onto the streets (see LEERING MAN). These men have been specially bred for centuries to have short or entirely non-existent necks. Fortunately for them their upper body strength allows them to peer over toilet doors for signs of wrong-doing despite their redundant necks. The average bouncer is easily confused, although not by logic or debate. Some breasts, or even a picture of some breasts, will distract this behemoth from his intentions.

UNINHIBITED DANCING MAN

This man is the happiest person in the club, as he is the only one who cannot see himself dancing. Everybody else is enormously embarrassed but too English to tell him he has the appearance of an electrocuted seal. Watch him for a while, until you are filled with existential angst over the sheer pointlessness of humanity, but long enough to observe at least one of the following:

☐	Singing incorrect song lyrics loudly	5 points
☐	Attempting, and failing, complicated dance move	10 points
☐	Knocking over someone's drink	5 points
☐	Knocking over someone's partner	10 points
☐	Knocking himself out	50 points
☐	Miniature vomit in mouth	20 points
☐	Maximum vomit out of mouth	50 points
☐	Unexpected urine-based incident	50 points

Culture and Cuisine

TOILET APOTHECARY

A sneaky, opportunistic man who lives in the toilets, surviving somehow only on a diet of lollipops and aftershave. He will watch your every move, from door to pissoir and has fucked up the drying machine for your hands. He offers you instead a paper towel, for which you must pay £1. After paying £15 to enter the sweaty shit-hole in the first place, £3.50 for a bottle of piss-warm lager or a toxic wine in a plastic glass, then £1.50 to hand over your jacket to a pissed-off teenager who will probably sell it, a paper towel for £1 actually begins to seem quite a bargain. Points are awarded depending on what is offered:

☐ Lollipop	5 points
☐ Aftershave	5 points
☐ Paper towel	5 points
☐ Condom	10 points
☐ Condom full of drugs	20 points
☐ Soup	25 points
☐ Marital advice	50 points
☐ Secret documents	100 points

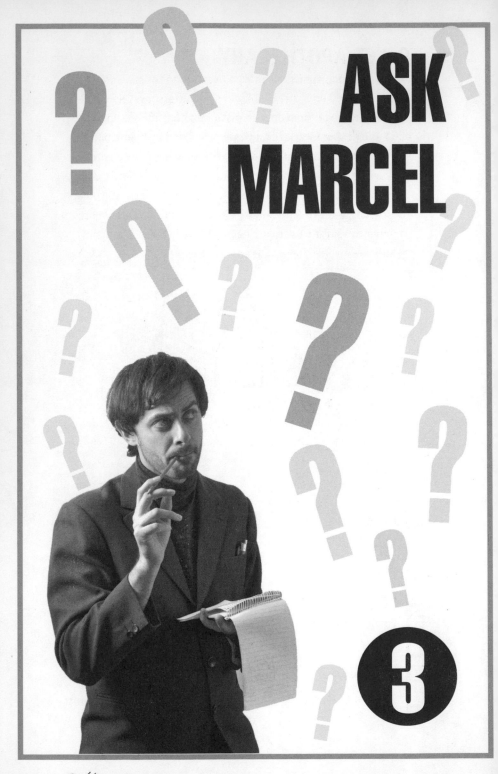

ASK MARCEL

3

Dear Marcel, I have been trying to spice up my love life for some time and have tentatively proposed the idea of anal sex to my wife of three years. To be honest, it's not something I considered before marriage, but all the guys in the lettings department have been raving about it. Every time she simply laughs it off as though I'm joking, but this has only made me want to pursue this activity with her all the more. Should I push the point (no pun intended) or just leave the matter alone? **Eddie Chambers, Leamington Spa**

Marcel Says: Firstly, I do not for one minute believe there was 'no pun intended' – I know the English too well for this to be true. And part of my knowledge of the English is a reluctance by the women of this country to indulge in 'the dirty love'. Where I am from this is considered a gift. To offer this to a woman of my town, for her it is like Christmas. For a woman of England, it is more like Hallowe'en. An entirely different festival.

It sounds to me like the problem is with both of you. It is not your fault that you are British, but try to be a bit less British about all of this. Perhaps you are not mentioning her derrière enough, so she may be self-conscious of this as a sexual avenue (pun intended). Try mentioning it as often as possible, she will soon give in. Persistence is everything, sir. *Vive la persistence!*

The English Language

'If a man is dead, say he is dead, not "late". Is it not bad enough already to be dead, without having one's punctuality questioned?'

Stolen French

As a generous nation, we have allowed many of our words to enter into the British language and enrich the vocabulary. You are welcome. Alas, you are not always so faithful to the meaning of the original, superior, word or phrase.

Café In France, 'café' translates literally as 'coffee', as that is chiefly what should be served there. In Britain, however, 'café' seems to translate as 'luke-warm food drowned in grease, salt and sauces of multiple lurid colours, consumed while loud men belch all around you, spouting factually dubious opinions they have gleaned from the day's tabloid.'

Déjà vu A very useful expression for the English, which they can re-use upon losing yet another sporting event at which their chances of victory have been absurdly over-hyped by the media.

Hors d'oeuvre In France, a light but carefully-prepared appetizer before a sumptuous banquet. Or in Britain, some undisclosed meat on a stick.

Burlesque Once a noble satirical art form in France, in Britain it is now largely just vulgar stripping. Just because something sparkly is hanging from your tits, this does not make it art. If I painted my balls in glitter they would still not be welcome at the local discotheque.

Décor The interior furnishings of a house or establishment. If an Englishman invites you to his house and mentions his 'décor' there is a 92 percent chance it is from Ikea. Inform them they should be using the Swedish 'inredningsstil', not the French.

Joie de vivre The spirit of living life to its most full. It is often difficult to see how this phrase has gained any such usage in Britain. For the French, whose lifestyle is regularly described as the best in

Europe, one can understand it – a 35-hour working week, 34 days holiday for those unlucky enough to be in an office job, and the most money spent on healthcare. In Britain, even your bars must create 'happy hours' to enforce joy on their customers.

Au naturel Often I have found myself with an English girl au naturel, only to find that, beneath her clothes, she is anything but naturel. That 'tan' has been applied with a paint brush or a jet spray (or, in some cases, it appears, simply a bucket), and between her legs, rather than a welcome mat I have been greeted instead by a bizarre vertical eyebrow, or Adolf Hitler's upper lip.

Apéritif In France: a small, strong alcoholic drink to stimulate one's appetite. The precursor to a sumptuous meal with excellent company. In Britain: a small, strong alcoholic drink to drop into another larger alcoholic drink. The precursor to a several more apéritifs, a fight and more apéritifs.

Double entendre A phrase we do not even use in France, having

surpassed such trivial humour some time ago. Supposedly a witty play-on-words which confounds the listener, it is in fact merely an excuse for a British person to raise their eyebrows and say 'ooh' at the words 'bush', 'hard' or 'portion'.

Objet d'art In France, a carefully-crafted masterpiece. In Britain, a dead animal in a glass case, a dirty bed or a glittery skull.

Ennui An expression of such life-sapping disinterest that the English language simply has no direct translation for it. It is appropriate for many a situation I have found myself in while in Britain, chiefly listening to any British conversation about immigrants, sporting superiority, or jingoist superiority in general. Or, in the case of a specific ill-timed visit to Ireland, a weekend-long discussion over a football referee's 'handball' decision, which I now refer to as 'Thierry ennui'.

Déjà vu A very useful expression for the English, which they can re-use upon losing another sporting event at which their chances of victory have been absurdly over-hyped by the media.

Mortgage Quite literally a 'dead pledge'. If only you had realized just how 'dead' these pledges were when your city bankers were playing around with money which technically did not exist ...

Corduroy 'The clothes of the king' originally, as such fabric was worn by royalty. In England corduroy garments are only worn by perverts and the unemployed. So, very little difference, I suppose.

Beef We give to you the word, you give it back to us insane and frothing at the mouth. *Merci bien*.

Adieu If you use this to say to someone goodbye, technically you are telling them to go to God, or in, simpler terms, 'go and kill yourself'. This is a phrase I often find myself using in ignorant English company, usually with a wry smile.

Negligée French term for a woman who neglects her appearance. In England, a woman believes this can be resolved by simply throwing on a light piece of fabric at bedtime. The French, of course, know this simply to be *mouton* dressed as *agneau*.

Denim Fabric originally 'de Nîmes', as it came from Nîmes. Had the manufacturers known what they had started, I think perhaps they would have stopped immediately. Anyone who believes the world to be a better place since the invention of dungarees requires examining.

Soupçon A very small amount of food, but also a word we use for suspicion. Fitting, as I am often served a suspiciously small amount of food at several British restaurants. The British, of course, will tell you that size is not everything, but with portions that small, I expect at least some flavour to go with them.

Aide-mémoire Something to assist one in remembering an important point. For example, daily news reports from an unnecessary war, reminding an ex-British leader that he probably made a very important wrong decision. Of course, instead of conflict, he most probably described it as 'aid' in his memoirs ... See also the French word 'charlatan'.

Words That Are Better in French

Pamplemousse – grapefruit
Only the most stubborn Briton
would deny that the word
'pamplemousse' is infinitely better
than 'grapefruit'. We know it is
a fruit and we know it is *not* a
grape. You are calling something
by a thing it is, and a thing it is
not. 'Pamplemousse' feels good
in the mouth, unlike the bitter
fruit itself, which should not be
associated with the noble grape.

**Bonhomme-de-neige –
snowman**
A 'good man of the snow' in
France, not just a 'snow man'.
When we construct him we are
proud of him. We build him up,
give him strong shoulders, a good
scarf and hat, and a pipe if he is
lucky. The British simply build an
effigy of a man and attack him
with snow until his head comes
off, like the brutish race they are.
This is a terrible way to go – to be
decapitated by your own balls.

**Allumé/déchiré/pompette –
rat-arsed/wrecked/wankered**
Sometimes in France a celebration
will escalate and *Monsieur
L'Alcool* will initiate this. This is a
perfectly acceptable instance for
a Frenchman to be taken over by
the grape. However, in Britain, to
be pushed beyond the threshold
of sobriety, any excuse is accepted
– perhaps there being nothing
to watch on the television,
celebrating the middle of the week
or a new flavour of crisp. Whatever
the reason, both the French and
the British know the effect it will
have upon them: a Frenchman is
said to be lit up, pumped or ripped
in two like a page of poetry; an
Englishman is seen to be like a
train wreck, a wanker or with the
face of a rodent's arse.

Papillon – butterfly
The French have produced a
wonderful onomatopoeic term
for this delicate and beautiful

creature, its name emanating perhaps from the rhythmic fluttering of its intricate, kaleidoscopic wings. In English, once again, a baffling combination of words has been cobbled together to name the poor insect. Butter leads to disease of the heart and a fly likes nothing more than to gather around shit. *'Merci l'Angleterre'*, whispers the papillon.

Coquette – slag

Ah, the 'fairer sex' as you say. A French woman can earn herself the accolade of 'coquette' by dressing in chic clothes and gliding through a room subtly diverting every man's attention. In Britain, a woman will push her tits into a bra one size too small, and paint enough make-up on her face to cover a hut. This will earn her the title of 'slag', a term also used for a waste product of coal production. Perhaps this is what fake tan is extracted from.

Saperlipopette! – blimey!

When faced with a surprising yet trivial matter – rain on a summer's day, the breaking of a mirror, one's wife having discovered the identity of one's lover(s) – the French prefer to deal with this using a nonsensical word that instantly takes the edge off the situation. The English, of course, overreact and choose instead words such as 'blimey', derived from 'God blind me!' How this request is supposed to help the situation is a mystery to me. If anything, such an action would simply make one's day considerably worse. Although I suppose one would not need to buy a new mirror.

Putain de bordel de merde! – Jesus fucking Christ!

For far more serious matters – e.g. discovering one's wife has taken a new lover – stronger words are used, of course. The English equivalent of *'putain de bordel de merde'* (whore from a shitty brothel) is 'Jesus fucking Christ!' At least whores from shitty brothels can be proved to exist (just ask me about an experience in Marseille in 2003). I say, if one is enraged, one is wasting words if choosing words describing mythical figures. Frankly, I am surprised this is still the fashion, since surely nobody to this day has been blinded by a thunderbolt after exclaiming 'blimey!'

What They Mean to Say

The English language is often associated with politeness, which certainly explains how the British Empire has got away with so much over the years, but look a little closer at every polite British utterance and you will see what they are really trying to say. The French tend to mean what they say and this directness will ensure you know their intentions, but with the British some decoding is required:

Pardon me – 'Fuck you'

This is a massively overused phrase in English, deployed to accompany a fart, a phone-call answered mid-conversation or a high-street collision (perhaps due to an attempt to multi-task the previous two). The British love to queue and 'pardon me' will certainly be applied to someone if queue etiquette is not adhered to by them, often spoken in an angry tone which immediately reveals the hidden message.

Oh, is that the time? – 'You boring fuck'

A British person may check their watch and pretend they have somewhere better to be (rarely true). It is generally considered a faux pas if the person uttering this rhetorical question is clearly not wearing a watch.

You're looking well – 'You fat fuck'

The British love their euphemisms for obesity: 'muffin tops', 'bingo wings', 'moobs', but please, let us call it what it is – FAT. There really is no excuse for this. British, instead of inventing new ways to describe this, you should be more French regarding this ever-expanding issue and view it as a crime against the eyes.

ASK
MARCEL

4

Dear Marcel, I have always considered myself a heterosexual man, but recently an experience at a party made me question this. Without going into too much detail, I ended up sharing a bed with a man and a woman, and awoke confused and slightly embarrassed. This is very out-of-character for me and I felt I should turn to a man of the world, such as yourself, for an opinion of where to go from here. **William N Taylor, Warninglid**

Marcel Says: I hope you are not simply using this column for the purpose of boasting. That is my job. Trust an Englishman to see this situation as a 'problem'. And to 'not go into too much detail'. Why not? That is the only reason the British read these advice columns anyway. So you may be bisexual? What is the problem here? You have just doubled your options at future parties.

Myself, I have only had gay experiences as part of an orgy, with no subsequent issues. In fact, afterwards it creates a rather wonderful atmosphere in which to discuss world politics. I am not sure, however, I could do sex face-to-face with just one other man (well, technically face-to-back-of-face – I know the logistics). For me, it is like the anchovy – I can eat one spread over a pizza, but one by itself is too much. As Baudelaire said, 'sexuality is the lyricism of the masses.' And what becomes of the man capable of singing only one set of lyrics? He is eventually either ignored, or beaten severely on long-distance transport by his fellow passengers.

As for the phrase 'man of the world', I have always found this a little bizarre. Are we not all men of the world? Or otherwise technically an alien.

[signature]

Afterword

Well, there it is. I hope you have read this book from cover to cover and taken notes. As France once again tops the polls for European quality of life, there should be little doubt that every word I have written is true. Do not despair, Britain, there is plenty of room for improvement. For all my misanthropy, I have faith in humanity to improve through the teachings of greater beings. And perhaps one day, simple Briton, you will visit our land at least partially prepared for the superior experience in store.

To conclude, in an ancient language that binds us, 'veni, vidi, tuam matrem feci, exii'.

À bientôt,

[signature] Lucont

Index

Previous Books by the Author

All of the following are now out of print, and very limited editions, as I do not wish to go along with the capitalist ethos pervading the world. They are perhaps available in antique bookshops and will cost several times more than the original price.

Ménage à Cinq A travelogue of my exploits around Europe in my early 20s, the title being a fairly good indicator of its tone.

Il Fait Boo – **Une histoire pour les enfants**
Banned in several countries, this hard-hitting horror tale for children is a must for parents wishing to scare their children into behaving. Its central character is the ghost of a murderer who eats children's souls.

Diagnosis: Merde A travelogue from a memorably appalling trip to the city of Los Angeles, encompassing all the vulgarities of the USA. Sadly, it is half the length of the original draft, due to various legal concerns, and every name had to be altered, even those of the sniffer dogs.

Whores d'Oeuvre An account of loose executive women in the City of London. The original title, 'Banque!', I deemed too sensationalist.

Les Seins Poétiques

A collection of poetic praise for the frontal bumps of ladies. Subjects' names have been changed, mainly because I could not remember all of them, but the sentiment remains the same. Contains 'The Tits of The Brits', 'Téton À Téton' and 'Breast(s) of Friends'.

Les Seins Poétiques
par Marcel Lucont

Poésie Sexy du W.C.
A sublime book of sex poetry set, and often written, within toilet facilities. Includes the classic '*Baise-moi Çe Soir Dans le Pissoir*'.

Marcel Lucont Merchandise

Womanizer de Marcel Lucont

A spray to get rid of excess women. Buy five bottles of Womanizer and get a free shitty stick.

Marcel Lucont condoms

What better talisman could you have during the act of sexual intercourse? I cannot be there to guide you in person, so this is the next best thing and an extra thrill for the woman of your affections.

Three different designs:
- The thumbs up
- The salute
- The dive

Four different flavours:
- Beaujolais (light, fruity)
- Pinot noir (medium, hint of plums)
- Bordeaux (full-bodied)
- Roquefort

Disclaimer: condoms are not a 100 percent guarantee against insemination. Marcel will have nothing to do with any children born as a result of wearing a Marcel Lucont condom.

Cigarette packet covers

Tired of being told by your government that your favourite pastime is killing you? Sick of feeling guilt for something that calms you down in this crazy modern world?

Well simply place these labels over your cigarette packet, to show the world how committed you are to this pursuit, in this age of over-enforced legislation.

- SMOKING CAN LEAD TO GREAT SEX
- SMOKING SHROUDS ME IN MYSTERY
- SMOKING IS BIG AND CLEVER
- CIGARETTES: SOMETHING ELSE WILL PROBABLY KILL ME FIRST
- SMOKING IMPROVES JAZZ

Acknowledgements

Merci ...

Alexis Dubus   Aruna Vasudevan

Charlotte Macey   Geraldine Timmins

Russell Garnett   Fliss Russell

Corrie McGuire   Louise Howells

Kate Parker   Pauline Lord

Amber Topaz   Lexi Bradburn

Sy Thomas   Ann Pidcock

Haydn Samuels   Amy Thornhill

Anna Victoria Izquierdo   Lynsey Dargue